# Mad About Us

How to honor your marriage by loving
your relationship

Doug McKinley, Psy.D.

*Mad About Us*
by Doug McKinley, Psy.D.

Printed in the United States of America

ISBN 1-594674-29-9



The anecdotes in this book are based on the author's research. In all cases, names and identifying information have been changed.

www.xulonpress.com

To my wife Jana
For seeing the potential of love in me,
and risking going on the adventure of love with me.

# Acknowledgments

It was said by Picasso, that *everything you can imagine is real.* I imagined writing this book and am very grateful to many people who assisted me in *making it real!*

First, my wife, Jana, patiently walked this journey with me from beginning to end. Your encouragement and love kept me going. My children, Seth and Megan, never doubted the completion of this book.

Don and Dorothy McKinley, my mom and dad, always believed I could achieve whatever I set out to do.

Heidi Akridge gave numerous hours of input to the initial editing process.

Debbie Reha, my assistant, did all the graphic design work. She knows my heart and steadily guides me to follow it.

Jennifer Fusco gave incredible guidance and counsel to the overall editing and layout. I could not have finished this project without her and Alex Lubertozzi from Prologue Publishing Services.

Karen Kochenburger and Xulon assisted me in getting this book into print.

I give heartfelt thanks to my friends and colleagues who made contributions to this book. Their comments were often very timely and helpful.

*Lastly, I want to thank the couples who have allowed me the honor of witnessing their marriages in the therapy and coaching process. Most of my discoveries came as a result of the many hours observing these couples fight for and design their marriage.*

# Contents

*Chapter One*

# Traffic Light Marriages

We were standing in the hotel lobby perplexed. On vacation and beginning our first day together, Jana and I had numerous options. Do we go to the beach together or get the groceries for the week? Perhaps Jana could go to the pool while I check on the costs to go scuba diving. I really don't enjoy lying on the beach, so I could make a tee time and play golf. While my wife and I enjoy going on vacation, we could easily have separate experiences and still call it togetherness. I have discovered that the way couples make decisions while on vacation, as well as in other situations, provide an inside look at their preferred style of interaction. This book will address my observations about how a couple's interaction style determines the type of intimacy they enjoy.

Some couples are too close, some are too distant, some need more intimacy, and others need more fun. While each couple I interview struggles with different aspects of marriage, every one of them would agree that each marriage is an undiscovered mystery.

*Mad About Us* is a raw perspective on the marriage relationship with a particular interest in the *us* development. The word "mad" has numerous meanings. Mad is quickly recognized by some couples as representing anger and frustration in their marriage. Mad also expresses hilarity and enthusiasm in marriages where couples experience fun and lightness.

While there are similarities in marriages, it is safe to say that no two marriages are alike. However, from both research and clinical experience, I've found that most couples fall into three categories based on their style of developing marital unity.

The three marriage types are:
Us marriages
Cooperative I marriages (CI)
Me marriages

Because no couple fits into any one style exactly, there are overlaps between types. The typical couple moves back and forth between marriage styles, depending on circumstances, awareness, and environmental stressors.

If you experience a unique connection and deep spiritual union with your mate, you may relate to the *Us Marriage* style. This marriage type provides couples with unity in mind and spirit. The relationship takes priority over individual needs. Us marriages cannot sustain unity continuously: they will find themselves shifting styles throughout the marriage. This will not discourage Us marriages because they know how to get reconnected.

If you are basically content in your marriage, most likely you will identify with the *Cooperative I Marriage*. This type of relationship is commonly viewed as a good marriage. Couples who work together well and avoid major conflicts are considered to have done well. Many couples are motivated and content to make each other happy. They long for a deeper connection that comes from the Us relationships, yet find themselves bogged down by the pace of life and the financial demands to stay ahead. There are many levels of this type of marriage. Some CI couples work hard to make their marriage fair, while others strive to become interested in having a peaceful relationship. The primary complaint of this marriage type is lack of intimacy.

If you experience stress or dissatisfaction in your marriage, or you are laboring to take care of yourself, then you are probably in a *Me Marriage*. The Me marriage type appears to be a default position. When you are struggling for common ground with your mate, the journey can lead to isolation. Yet, if you make the effort to cooperate with your spouse, you may generate enough interest to begin working together. This can prepare the relationship for negotiating toward a give-and-take process.

Think of these relational behaviors as compared to a traffic signal:

The red light signifies the Me marriage
The yellow light signifies the Cooperative I marriage
The green light signifies the Us marriage

Traffic light colors hold specific meaning to automobile drivers. I have transferred those same meanings to the three types of marriages described. Just as stoplights mediate traffic, this book will illustrate how couples mediate relational demands by their marriage styles. The majority of married couples interact in the CI marriage style. Consequently, I am suggesting that as you travel the highways of your married life, you pay attention to the signals that indicate your interaction style. When red lights pop up, stop what you are doing and reflect on what needs to change to prevent selfishness. When you notice yellow lights, proceed with caution and acknowledge that you may need to slow down and rethink what you are doing. When you have green lights, proceed with confidence and enjoy the ride.

In an Us marriage, couples are free to move around without concern of being attacked, blindsided, or punished. The green light in marriage refers to the freedom couples experience as they enjoy safety in the relationship. When drivers see the green light they have confidence the path they are taking is clear. Likewise, Us couples are free to pass through difficult intersections in life because the relationship is prepared for them.

The yellow light represents the Cooperative I marriage, indicating there are times you can proceed and others you need to be prepared to stop what you are doing. Many times, driving through a yellow light can be risky. Other times, the yellow light indicates a change is going to happen soon, so proceed with caution. The CI couple experiences similar disruptions in the flow of their marriage. For them, things may be going fine, and then, suddenly things change. This could be the arrival of a new baby, change of jobs, or unforeseen financial challenges. When couples are operating in this type of marriage style, they will experience hesitation and safety concerns more often than the green light marriages.

Everyone knows what a red light in a traffic signal indicates. Unfortunately, not every couple realizes their marriage is in danger. Me marriages remind me of the meaning drawn from the red light. I often tell these couples to stop proceeding with their current behavior, because there is a high probability of serious damage if they don't. Like with traffic, marriages need signals that warn of oncoming problems that will directly impact their lives. Couples that operate from a Me perspective often reflect what happens to drivers who run red lights. Sometimes there is immediate tragedy, sometimes people get punished, and other times they get away with it, leaving others in danger because of their recklessness.

The next three sections address in more detail the behavioral patterns, philosophies, and pros and cons of each marriage type. As noted earlier, couples may have a typical style, but they will move back and forth between styles as situations change. Look for your primary style and ask yourself how that style is working for you. The remaining chapters of this book will address how to get the best out of the CI and Us marriage style while addressing ways to avoid the Me marriage style.

**The Green Light Marriage (The Struggle for Meaning)**

The Us marriage type is based on the principle of unity. Two unique individuals with dominant traits are blended to create another unique personality that is non-dominant, the Us. Notice the green light that symbolizes this marriage style is not a primary color. Green results when two primary colors are blended. The safety couples experience in this unity style is unparalleled because the relationship is a collaboration of two people, whereby their individual "color" is unrecognizable.

Partners in Us marriages don't keep score because they are on the same team. They may notice individual stats, but only to encourage one another. Us marriages generate confidence and grow strong individuals. Because the "I's" surrender to the Us, individuals can relax and enjoy the multiplied energy the marriage creates for them.

For this to work, each partner gives to the other from the love they have, rather than to get the love they want. Couples who live this way find marriage rewarding and energizing. These green light couples are love-filled, life-tested, and deeply invested in their love connection. Several years ago, Jana and I observed an Us couple that suffered a tragedy in their family, one of those "things that aren't supposed to happen to us." Sadly, it did happen and they were forced to accept it and adapt. Their courage and will to keep a healthy relationship was extremely encouraging to us. I heard words like, "We trust God," and, "It's awful, but we'll get through it," as they told us about their struggles. I can tell that because they went through the experience together, this mentor couple will be able to absorb any blow that life throws them. The motivation of the Us marriage is to invest in—and draw from—the relationship, rather than from each other.

Us marriages grow because of love, rather than working hard for a love relationship. One simple example of this principle is found in finance and investing. Experts often suggest that you must let your money work for you. Those who understand this principle put their money into mutual funds or stocks and wait for their investment to pay them dividends. Rather than spending all their money each month, they put some of it into this "place" and hope for the best. In other words, if you keep giving to a productive investment, it will grow and pay dividends beyond the current earning capacity of the dollars invested. When Jana and I sat down with a financial planner, he laid out the numbers for us, and it was staggering how much money we could accumulate if we started investing right then! Thanks to his advice, Jana and I are building a nest egg.

Marriages are no different. Start donating to an Us account and watch the marriage pay you dividends beyond the value of the donations. This is a simple process, but hard to trust. When a couple has money, it's easier to spend it. They work hard for every dollar and want the payoff as quickly as possible. Likewise, investing in the third entity of the relationship, the Us, is risky. Couples are afraid they may lose their investment, or that one partner may donate more than the other; particularly those in a CI marriage.

Trust is implicit in this process.

I occasionally work with people who are unwilling to surrender their individual agendas to grow their relationship. The most common reason is fear. One couple I counseled was convinced that they would have to give up their careers for each other. When they realized a change in their personal career paths was necessary to save the marriage, they terminated therapy and filed for a divorce. An underlying reason for marital breakdown is the fear of losing control. The Us marriage gives the couple the ability to transcend their fear through secure love, unconditional acceptance, and freedom from competition and selfishness. Obviously, achieving the Us connection is not easily maintained for long periods of time. However, I work with many couples that find this type of marriage compelling. They learn to surrender to the marriage, focus on the relationship, and soon realize the benefits. These couples are discovering ways to manage pain from the past, communicate with renewed motivation and hope, and look forward to cocreating a preferred future.

In Philippians 3:12–14, the apostle Paul is speaking about being focused on being faithful to God, and provides a process that mirrors the journey of an Us marriage: "Not that I have already attained all this, or have already been made perfect, but I press on to take hold of that for which Christ Jesus took hold of me. Brothers, I do not consider myself yet to have taken hold of it. But one thing I do: Forgetting what is behind and straining toward what is ahead, I press on toward the goal to win the prize for which God has called me heavenward in Christ Jesus."

***Image of Us***

When you think about married people, you usually describe their individual characteristics rather than describing their relationship. Jay and Cheryl have a strong marriage. I describe Jay as quiet and strong and Cheryl as creative and energetic. When they are socializing with other couples, Jay is laid back and observant, while Cheryl is the life of the party. Because their individual traits stand out, it's easy to overlook their marriage relationship. Often, couples are addressed by the male's last name, as in, "Hey, the McKinley's are here!" The couple image is unique. The more ways a couple exposes their marriage relationship, the more nurtured it becomes. In Jay and Cheryl's case, their marriage values family, kindness, and loyalty.

When holding Mad About Us seminars, I ask couples to identify characteristics that describe their relationship. At first they find it difficult, because they usually don't have a relationship language in place. Couples first address their individual characteristics and then work their way into relationship descriptions. As difficult as it may be describing "Us" traits, doing so reminds couples to live *out* of the relationship rather than live *for* it.

When I am facilitating a seminar, I have couples answer some questions regarding their interests and relational activities. I have included the exercise for you as a way to discover your Us knowledge.

***Us Indicators***

When a couple marries, they dream about being a part of a growing relationship. Soon after the honeymoon, they begin dividing the Us into domestic roles, careers, and so on. Do we really stop and think about the fact that we are developing, growing, and encouraging a whole other entity? I propose that there are three of us. There is the me; there is the you; and there is the Us. To illustrate, I, Doug McKinley, do not like romantic comedies. I would never purposely bring home a romantic comedy. I like movies where things blow up and alien creatures are often the main characters. While I don't care for romantic comedies, Us loves them. When Us is watching a romantic comedy, there is something about the way Jana smiles, the feeling we have together, and the discussions that happen because of it, that Us really likes. That's not to say I just watch the movie because I have to. It doesn't mean it's my turn to accommodate. This is a completely different experience. Knowing it's not my favorite thing to do, Jana will say, "Is it too slow? Is it okay? What do you think?" The Us part of me is really enjoying the movie, although I would not watch it alone or with my friends. I respond with a gentle nod, implying I'm with her all the way. This gives Us a great time together. Because I am married and have created this Us place in our life together, it is a completely different and enjoyable experience.

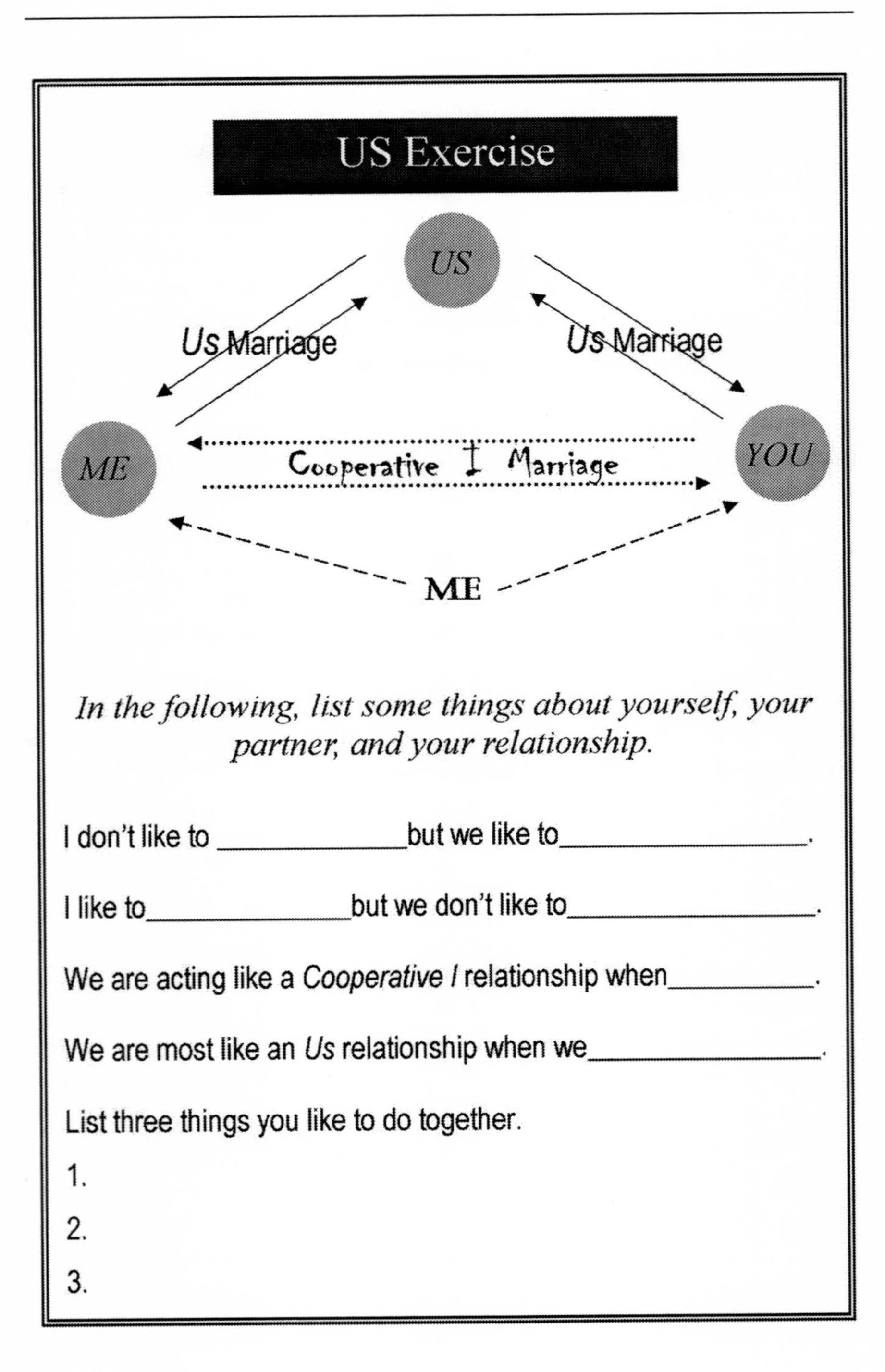


## US Exercise

*In the following, list some things about yourself, your partner, and your relationship.*

I don't like to ______________ but we like to ___________________.

I like to________________ but we don't like to__________________.

We are acting like a *Cooperative I* relationship when___________.

We are most like an *Us* relationship when we_________________.

List three things you like to do together.

1.

2.

3.

The Us is nurtured by both of us, together, but it also must be fed by the individuals. For example, both men and women struggle with visual temptations. Being in a marriage relationship requires self-control in this area. When I am confronted with visual temptation, the commitment to Us serves as a reminder to steer clear. A few years ago I came out of a workshop in Denver, Colorado, feeling tired. I had been contemplating marriage relationships and was thinking about the Us concept. While I was walking down the street, I saw an attractive woman. I immediately said to myself, "She is pretty, but dwelling on that would not be good for my Us relationship." I was one thousand miles away from home, staying in a hotel alone. My commitment to Us had to be brought back into focus. Avoiding these kinds of traps is one reason why our marriage continues to grow and work. Us is very important to Jana and me. The things we share in this relationship overpower many of the "I" things that I enjoyed before marriage. I have to discipline my mind to remember that my needs are not the only star on the flag.

Although the Us relationship is crucial, each person in the marriage must maintain their own identity. There are things I enjoy doing that Us does not like. Jana is not particularly competitive. I am passionate about sports. I especially enjoy fierce competition. Her sacrifice to the Us relationship allows me to enjoy sports without feeling threatened. That part of me, as an individual, is very important—I will keep playing as long as it doesn't impact the Us negatively. The Us becomes endangered when the "I" wants to play softball four nights a week and basketball three days a week. When the Us is adversely impacted, both "I's" suffer.

Jana enjoys some activities and hobbies that are not interesting to me at all. Sometimes I forgo my interests to support her in getting her needs met. This is a CI behavior that is often timely and needed. At one of my workshops, a husband explained this concept clearly by sharing, "I enjoy eating at Hooters Restaurant, but Us doesn't." This example provides a humorous perspective of the differences between Us and CI interests. Some activities you will invest in are not Us activities, but are still important to the Us. When Jana comes to my games, she is supporting me, which is different than supporting Us. Us activities are mutually enjoyable to both parties. They are initiated and enjoyed by the relationship.

***Surrendered I's***

This whole concept boils down to one simple step. Simple, but powerful: We must surrender ourselves to the relationship. For instance, when an acquaintance says, "Jana seems like a nice person," and I respond by agreeing with that comment, I am responding for Us. In other words, when Jana is complemented, I am complemented as well. We are much more together, than either of us could be on our own. I have accomplished far more than I imagined because of my connection to Jana and my surrendering to Us. Writing this book is a perfect example. I simply could not have written it without her. Likewise, if someone says to me, "Your wife is nosey," it reflects on Us in a negative way. I need to respond with a comment that suggests those types of observations are untrue and unwanted and dismiss myself from the conversation. We are together and our individual expressions about each other impact who we are as a couple.

You're only as "good" as the blend of both of you. I hear comments made about other couples such as, "How could she stay married to that creep?" These comments imply that he may be a creep, but for sure *she* is stupid. Just remember, when you're married, you're not alone. The woman doesn't "stay" with a creep, she is in a relationship with him. A decision to live in an Us relationship requires partners to think for two.

I advise partners to check in regularly, "Hey, how is our Us doing?" While answers may initially be, "I can tell you are doing well," or "Work is hectic," partners who continue to probe will begin to get Us answers. Each partner must actively pursue Us preservation, rather than just encouraging individuality.

Our culture teaches us to become very skilled and reactive to preserving "I." There's nearly an epidemic against the Us: society—driven by media—sends messages constantly about "I" survival. The slogan "Be all you can be" prevails. Often the Us is not only ignored, but is also destroyed inadvertently. There are lawyers for divorcing individuals, but very little protects the union of marriage. It's a great challenge to save the Us relationship and maintain its boundaries. We understand spousal abuse, child abuse, and emotional abuse, but there isn't a language yet for relational abuse.

Recently, I spoke with a woman going through divorce. I asked if she understood that divorce is a lawsuit against their relationship? In essence, the husband was saying, "I don't want Us anymore." Divorce is a lawsuit and a separation from the Us. When one person becomes selfish within the marriage, the Us relationship is under attack, neglected, or abused. When one person pulls out of an Us relationship, it leaves a huge void for one person in a place where it takes two to fight for success.

When you get married, you surrender the "I," and say, "I commit to a different path than my selfish nature would follow. I desire this surrender because I envision greater happiness in what we two can create together." In surrendering to marriage, partners will enjoy an unrivaled relationship. Like the name of a popular song by an old group, Champagne, consider a new motto for your marriage: *How About Us*?

**The Yellow Light Marriage (The struggle for equality)**

Yellow Light marriages, or Cooperative I (CI) marriages, are based on logical policies of give and take. They are best described as fair marriages that follow a quid-pro-quo, or "something for something" behavior. CI marriages are motivated by the need to exchange favors.

The color yellow in a traffic signal is the caution light. It signals you to make a judgment before proceeding, by considering all the facts. When you drive through a yellow light you must be confident that those around you understand your intentions and are willing to cooperate with you. For your safety, you rely on another person's interpretation of the occurring events. Likewise, in marriage you must consider how your partner responds to experiences differently than you.

CI marriages depend on cooperation, because without it there are no clear directions. When cooperation is high, the couple thrives. When cooperation is hard to come by, the couple battles. This type of marriage is only as successful as the couple's willingness to be fair. When they have learned that sharing and working together can benefit both sides, CI marriages enjoy a comfortable coexistence.

The CI relationship, however, promotes scorekeeping. A "tit for tat" philosophy may start out as fun and games but it soon creates anxiety about fairness. When fairness is continually in question, the relationship is drained of precious life-giving resources. Rodney Dangerfield once joked, "We sleep in separate rooms, we have dinner apart, we take separate vacations—we're doing everything we can to keep our marriage together." Cooperation between spouses is a necessary ingredient for marriage. Of the three types, the CI marriage represents the largest number of marriages.

Although you may want the Us connection, you are hoping to at least feel like a team. I work with couples who are actively searching for or maintaining the Cooperative I style. One couple, Dan and Shirley, are so cooperative they haven't had sex for more than ten years. Their marriage is based on the principles of fairness. He works full-time and does so willingly. She works part-time as a beautician and raises their four children. He is passive and compliant. She is energetic and cooperative. They are both very nice people who get along very well. All their friends say they have a great marriage. Yet, Shirley feels no passion with Dan. She loves him like a brother.

Dan doesn't see a problem with their marriage, except that Shirley is not happy. Dan is content just managing day-to-day operations. He works hard, solving problems all day. He is highly valued as a computer troubleshooter. Because he responds well to crisis, he is well liked and has a great work arrangement. Shirley was hoping marital counseling would change her feelings from pitiful to passionate. She wanted therapy to help Dan discover his real self. Her belief was that his discovery might re-ignite her passion. Without mutual goals, interests, and values, marriage can end up feeling empty.

Love between couples is difficult to explain because there are varying beliefs about it. Psychologist Robert Sternberg designed a theoretical three-part model for love. According to his love model, there are three components: *motivational*, *emotional,* and *mental.*[1] This love model gives couples a language to discuss and measure love in a practical manner.

Too often, love is misunderstood. Some couples randomly give love to their relationship hoping for something to connect, like trying to get marbles into a jar by dropping them from three feet above. You can drop them all at once and hope for the best, or you can strategically place each marble over the jar and drop it in. It is easy to see how the odds of success may increase using the latter method. The CI marriage is built by communicating about what love is, clarifying individual needs, and discovering ways to meet them. This type of interaction, compared to Me marriage, provides a higher potential for love needs between partners to get met.

***Passion: The Motivational Part of Love***

I read a story recently about a special marriage. I found myself intrigued by the author's energy and passion for his wife. David dedicated Wednesdays to intentionally keep his romance alive. During his courtship with Patricia, he could hardly wait until the weekends to be with her. To bridge the gap between weekends, he discovered a way to connect during the week. Every Wednesday he foraged through greeting cards to find one that appropriately shared his feelings about his girlfriend. David claims he has not missed a Wednesday since that first card. He'd been married fourteen years when he wrote that story. He spent countless hours in card shops all those years thinking about, dreaming about, and anticipating a passionate connection with his wife.

Passion drives us to do strange things. In fact, the term *passion* means suffering. Compassion means co-suffering. Think of all the songs that refer to love as "hurting" such as the old tune by Roberta Flack, "Killing Me Softly." The drive to mate with the opposite sex is natural and strong. Paul Pearsall in, *The Ten Laws of Lasting Love* maintains that our brain does not first think of love. He says, "Our brains have minimal standards. They are satisfied with merely staying alive. Our brain's first mission is *not* to think or to love but to keep its life support system—the body—functioning. It is stimulated and alerted by the four F's—'fighting, fleeing, feeding, and sex'."[2] These four drives can serve as a reminder of the powerful influences the passion part of love have on a relationship, especially the last one! Pearsall goes on to say, "The mind wants much more out of the spirit's brief journey through humanhood than living. It is dedicated to the four F's of 'fleeing, forgiving, flourishing, and forever,' and it is in search of another mind to think about love with."[3]

John Eldredge wrote in his book, *Wild at Heart*, that men have three primary desires.[4] They want a battle to fight, an adventure to live, and a beauty to rescue. Love stories depict men traveling across continents, fighting fierce animals, and drowning in cold waters to save their lovers. Eldredge maintains women have three similar desires. They want to be fought for, to be on an adventure with, and to be seen as the beauty to be delighted in.

Passion is that magnetic aspect of love that pulls us toward one another. What is it in your marriage that causes that kind of energy shift? For love to be fully experienced, the passion part of the love equation is as important as the emotional and mental expressions. Passion is the fuel that keeps love running while sex, attraction, romance, and affection are the substance of the fuel. Think of passion as the "hot" side of the love triangle.

***Intimacy: The Emotional Part of Love***

Wanting to know your partner deeply is the first step to real intimacy. I'm confused by the absence of this desire in couples. It's almost as if the decision to marry is based on availability or timing rather than intimate understanding. Some men are more motivated to know how a television works before buying it than how their partner works before marrying her. Men will spend hours researching magazines, talking with friends, and consulting with experts before buying cars or electronics. When they are asked to go to five premarital counseling sessions, they moan over the waste of time. Do they think there's a money-back guarantee? Women, however, will spend hours discussing their boyfriends' most detailed qualities, but go out and buy the first car they think is cute. We're just wired differently.

Like any investment you make in a product, relationships require learning about the product, researching the best ways to utilize it, knowing how it works, and enjoying its purpose for being. Couples who talk about their needs, wishes, and dreams will begin to feel close. A primary purpose for marriage is to share your life with another person. This happens as each of you listens, talks, and explores your lives with one another.

Intimacy is the part of love that is best described as warmth, closeness, and familiarity. In nature, two particles cannot merge unless they are softened. Steel must be put to flame to be shaped, clay must be moistened, butter has to melt, and couples need warmth. When a couple attempts to build a marriage based solely on willpower and passion, it's like putting two hard pieces of wood together with nails. They appear to be joined, yet one good blow of a hammer can separate them. Intimate couples blend like fine jewelry. If you want love to last, you must become so intertwined that the blows of life won't pull you apart.

Intimacy is the marital glue that keeps the whole relationship together. A warm, trusting relationship lends itself to those gentle, secure feelings of love that are prevalent when the passion isn't burning. A marriage without intimacy can be calculated and stiff. Intimate couples are more likely to work through conflicts, make better joint decisions, and generally get along better during the mundane activities of daily life. You will want to know your partner in this way if your goal is to experience love emotionally.

***Commitment: The Mental Part of Love***

The choice to love is as powerful as the feeling. I remember choosing to love Jana. She was at the top of my list of possible mates when I was a junior in college. A mentor and I discussed the types of women that would be good for me to date. Attraction (passion) dominated most of our discussions; nevertheless, we still attempted to address the problem logically. I thought about dating differently as my years at college shortened. I began to realize that pure passion wouldn't be enough to select a *lifetime* mate. When two people make a decision to marry, there are many negotiations involved. I wrestled with the need to be physically attracted to my mate and my desire to enjoy being with her in everyday situations. I had questions such as, Is it more important to marry a beautiful babe or a fabulous friend? Perhaps the answer isn't *either/or,* but *and.*

Being committed to love requires active engagement of the mind. What does loving your mate look like? Are you willing to make the sacrifices necessary for a relationship to thrive? Are you making a lifetime commitment? Most divorced couples I work with assure me they never thought about divorce before the affair, the bankruptcy, the child, or whatever crisis brought them to that point. They began to question their decision to love by asking themselves, Was I ever really in love? The mental decision to love guides couples when the passion and emotion sides of the triangle are in doubt. The mind is capable of sorting out mixed feelings and chemically induced behavior. In fact, the mind can be trained to serve as the gatekeeper for the struggles found in all relationships. As a rudder guides a ship, your mind directs the passion and intimacy of your marriage. Having clear goals will assist couples in addressing each trial and celebrating each victory. The commitment to love is a powerful force that, with reason and discipline, allows marriage to last a lifetime.

Most couples love by trial and error. The initial obstacles of gender, personality, and social differences alone are overwhelming. Most young people do not have solid relationship skills when they begin a relationship, so most of us learn on the job! Without direction, love can be a mystery without any clues. Breaking down love into these three components of passion, intimacy, and commitment can enlighten and empower couples to harness, feed, and choose their loving relationship. Some trial and error in marriage is inevitable because of our unique differences, but love is definable with this triangle model.

The CI couple is preoccupied with working out the balance of these three aspects of love. Everything is good when one or two sides of love are flowing. The idea of having all three love needs met is an unforeseeable stretch. This couple is happy with what they get. Why should they complain when other couples are fighting constantly with lies, selfishness, and game-playing? Often, the CI couple feels fortunate among other couples to have such a workable relationship.

**The Red Light Marriage (The Struggle with Selfishness)**

When you reach a stoplight, the first thing you look for is the color. The red light is located at the top and we associate that light with stopping. I have found that many couples are doing things that make me want to stand up and say, "Red light, red light, red light!" The reason for my internal outburst is that the primary goal for partners in this arrangement—the Me marriage—is to get their own needs met. To them, marriage is a contest for personal satisfaction. Being satisfied in this relationship pertains to what *I get* from the marriage, rather than what *I can do* for the marriage. Only the toughest of these marriages survive, but not without suffering by both parties. A good example of this marriage taken to its extreme is the book and movie, *The War of the Roses*, in which both partners ended up dead rather than either one "losing" the contest. The red light behavior prevents growth because activities that don't have "I am going to benefit" written all over them are forbidden. I have observed many partners who merely exist in this type of marriage. They are disappointed in the relationship and usually find the whole process of simple communication more work than it's worth.

I remember one couple, Joe and Sara, who came to therapy because Joe had been having an Internet affair. He decided to take the affair to the next level, meeting his cyber friend in person. They spent several weekends together over a six-month period. In the meantime, Sara found enough clues to Joe's indiscretion to confront him. He denied everything. Sara was livid that he wouldn't admit to it, and she claimed her right to revenge. They were locked in a Me-marriage battle with no solutions because neither could get what they wanted. If Joe apologized, Sara would have to deal with the pain of forgiving him and moving toward reconciliation. If Sara forgave Joe, he would have to confront the reasons why he sought out a lover in the first place. While Joe didn't want Sara and she didn't want him, neither wanted a divorce. They talked about visions of a unified marriage, but only from selfish perspectives.

The Me couple cannot picture a team approach to their relationship. They only understand power and control. This tug-of-war is the basis of their connection. Whoever is in control gets what they want for a while, until the other gains more power. Joe and Sara had no comprehension of working together. Therefore, this new conflict was just another battle in the war, using different weapons. Me marriages escalate out of control until one person wins. That's the unwritten deal. When these couples seek counseling, they're not looking for a mediator; they're looking for a referee. Joe and Sara didn't want change; they wanted me to declare a "winner." Simply put, a red light marriage cannot grow because the inherent intention is to protect and preserve the individual.

The first recorded marriage relationship can be found in a very familiar setting. The story about this couple provides relevant information about self-protection. The Bible's Adam and Eve had the perfect marriage yet found a way to mess it up. It must have been blissful times for the two honeymooners. (Some would say, it had to be awesome without in-laws!) Although they had responsibilities, they had no self-consciousness; no "battle of the sexes," no hate. Only one rule governed their existence in this blissful environment.

In Genesis 2, it states, "When they ate the forbidden fruit, immediately they were aware of their nakedness." This sudden awareness becomes one answer to why making an Us marriage today is so difficult. Mankind became ashamed for the first time, thus beginning our never-ending neurosis about our bodies and souls. This emotional disturbance has no medication, no new psychotherapy techniques, and no program that can remedy the problem. It is my conviction that only Christ can heal us from the damage that experiment caused. My experience tells me that without the grace of God, our work would be far more difficult.

The Bible says Adam and Eve covered their loins with fig leaves. I have always wondered why the First Couple covered themselves in that way? Out of all body parts, why did they cover these parts instead of their faces, as some people do when they are embarrassed?

One theory is that they no longer felt freedom and acceptance, so they covered up what was most different about them. That feeling is prominent in our culture today. When we don't feel similar to other people, we tend to hide those aspects of ourselves that are different. When we have unpopular opinions, we don't express them freely because we don't want to be different. Adam and Eve were faced with the same powerful fears that I find in my work with couples. Couples who cannot overcome these fears remain in the Me marriage style. This style is loaded with emotional traps and the fears of being unloved, of being rejected, and of being insignificant.

***The Fear of Being Unloved***

The perception of being loved in our culture tends to be based on how we look. Consequently, physical appearance often becomes an obsession. Fear begins with feeling exposed. We are afraid to be ourselves because we think others won't love us if they know us as deeply as we know ourselves. Exposure leads to feelings of inadequacy. So the only answer is to hide behind a false image that "looks good" to others. Image management becomes the priority over honesty and character.

In some marriages, couples can be naked together, yet they are afraid of being emotionally exposed. Being physically vulnerable is not the problem: being emotionally vulnerable to each other's secrets and fears is what scares them most. The word naked evokes fear and excitement in most couples' minds. Early in marriage we discover nakedness from a physical perspective. This is challenging enough to overcome.

When I was a child, we lived in a small Indiana town just miles from a place called Naked City. My parents told me not to go there because of its reputation. So, like most obedient adolescent boys, my friends and I didn't visit Naked City openly, we just sneaked through the woods to its barrier fence and looked in. I remember feeling quite strange inside, hoping to catch a glance of a naked woman but also afraid I was doing something wrong. The tension of excitement and fear was overwhelming. When we went to the "city" barely peering over the fence, we heard voices. As the excitement built, I began to feel a little weird. Just as we hoped, three naked women came strolling near. At first I was stunned that they were really walking around naked. But even more stunning was the obvious fact that they were my mother's age, or older! My curiosity was replaced with, "Oh, my!" This mirrors some couples' experience with emotional and physical nakedness.

We live in a culture that profits from exposing perfect body parts. Companies use shock and sex to sell products because we are lured by lust. This terrible inequality between perfect images and reality has created havoc in our sexual relationships. When Adam and Eve ate the fruit and realized what they had done, they felt afraid for the first time. In turn, they tried to cover up the truth about themselves rather than face it. Most people are nervous about what people will think of their flaws. We need courage to confront the natural desire to conceal and cover up the truth when it comes to our blemishes. The irony is, the only way to overcome fear is to face it. Feeling loved is a wonderful thing, but to experience it we must become courageous enough to accept and reveal who we really are.

***The Fear of Being Rejected***

Rejection is one of those dreaded feelings that stems from the idea someone has "found me out." One of the contributing factors to low self-esteem and that expands the fear of rejection is comparison. Nathaniel Brandon, author of *The Six Pillars of Self-Esteem*, maintains, "The tragedy of many people's lives is that they look for self-esteem in every direction except within, and so they fail in their search."[5] Most people probably struggle with this because it's natural to seek approval from others and avoid being "found out." When we gain the approval of our peers (no matter the cost) we avoid the difficult process of being honest with ourselves.

When this "pleaser" mentality occurs between husband and

wife, the results can be devastating. One partner controls the other with opinion alone. The weaker person inevitably becomes insecure and ineffective as a partner because he or she is not true to their own values. A Me marriage feeds off this one-up–one-down principle.

You have heard it is natural to fear rejection. I wonder if it isn't foolish to ignore and miss the opportunity to learn from rejection? Some people think that rejection is the worst possible psychological experience. I have found that rejection is useful feedback for people who want to grow. Those who aren't open to self-awareness are being selfish in some ways. I am not saying I am looking forward to hearing my wife reject my proposal for buying a new car, for example, but when she does, I have a choice as to how I react to her rejection. Likewise, you can learn valuable lessons from people who reject you.

If you commit to a growing relationship, wouldn't you want to be willing to risk rejection? Being rejected by your partner momentarily, could lead to a closer connection later. Relationship growth cannot occur unless you face your fear of being rejected. If you are willing to overcome your need for approval and are true to your values, your marriage has a chance to grow. If you view approval as the only answer, you're likely to remain stuck in a struggle for self-protection.

Adam and Eve covered their hips after eating the fruit, and, realizing their differences, they began the debilitating habit of comparison. You tend to conceal your thoughts and feelings around people who don't share your views on things. You do not want to appear different so you tend to reveal yourself to those who agree with you. This psychological barrier is common in all ranks of society. From childhood through aged adults, people report struggling with all forms of self-comparisons.

Gender differences have become the focus of comparison for businesses, marriages, friendships, and organizations. Although each gender offers different but equally valuable gifts, our culture judges them for observable parity. For instance, in human service professions, men are expected to be more sensitive and soft. In business, women are required to be more decisive and strong. Many individuals are able to succeed in their careers without compromising their natural abilities. Their success should be your model. That model begins with knowing your gifts and accepting your limitations.

Regardless of gender, you are free to express those gifts meaningfully in all facets of life. Your gifts are unique and cannot be measured against any standards but your own.

Gender differences are to the human race what Baskin Robbins is to ice cream. This specialty ice cream restaurant, promotes 31 flavors to entice consumers to buy from them because of their variety—they will have the flavor each different customer desires. Like flavors of ice cream, gender differences offer a variety of different tastes that need not be compared but enjoyed for what they are. I am sure God had good reason for providing such a contrast when designing his creatures. I imagine he knew we would need to learn how to laugh at ourselves, to avoid being too self-focused. I heard that when God created the world, he made man and woman. Then, to keep the whole thing from collapsing, he invented humor. We would benefit by laughing about our differences and enjoy the spice that variety brings to our lives.

***The Fear of Being Unimportant***

Have you ever felt like your opinion, contribution, or your presence didn't matter? I observed an exchange between Noel and Jan that promoted this feeling. I named their exchange "The Blue Ribbon Game." Their game was based on arrogance and competition. The goal was to keep the opponent from being right. Playing the game kept them from improving communication and enjoying their relationship. We worked on empathy in the hopes they would understand each other better. When I finally got them to stop arguing, I asked them a question. "What makes each of you think you're entitled to be treated better?" Their responses were stunning and humorous.

Noel said he was more mature than Jan, so his shortcomings should be overlooked. He concluded this because she gets hysterical. She attacks with her requests, and she screams and throws fits when she doesn't get what she wants. Her emotional outbursts are frequent and furious. Noel believes she is obviously immature and should be considered the inferior competitor.

Jan's argument is that she does everything for Noel, so he is in her debt. She maintains the house, cooks all the meals, and manages social events. She considers herself the superior competitor because he is obviously incompetent and irresponsible. He doesn't care about the marriage, so he is a real "jerk" and unworthy of the ribbon.

Each of them believed they were better than the other. The competition for first place was obvious. They both wanted to feel important and were not getting that validated in a manner acceptable to their insecurities.

When I got them to verbalize what they'd been thinking, I noticed a slight smile break on their faces. The recognition of their absurd beliefs left them feeling vulnerable and embarrassed because they saw their own selfishness. Nevertheless, they were stuck in a contradictory pattern. They had to overcome their fears of being unimportant for the games to stop. I wish I could tell you they succeeded in overcoming their selfishness, but they are still stuck and unable to grow beyond their need to feel important and superior. When this trap is present, the couple must shift to validating each other or they will maintain their Me marriage struggle. Selfishness is the motivator that makes this game so damaging to relationships.

My own sense of importance was shaped in part by competitive games. During my school-age years I lived for playing football, basketball, and baseball. Sports helped me mature and developed my solid work ethic. Consequently, I recall being taught in football that clear sportsmanship and clean competition were valuable. I respected many of my coaches for teaching me a healthy balance between winning and fair play. Unfortunately, not everyone felt this way. One day after a football game, we were viewing films. I made a great defensive play where I sacked the quarterback for a seven-yard loss. After the play, I reached down and extended my hand to the guy to help him up after I had just flattened him. My coach was furious with me. He said, "McKinley if you ever do that again I will kick your butt!" What are you, some kind of wimp?" I stopped doing that little deed, of course, but I remember thinking his tactics were shallow. He was not only focused on winning, but also driven to prove his superiority by shaming his opponents. In retrospect, that wasn't teaching good sportsmanship at all. Looking back, I wonder if this tough-minded approach worked for him in his marriage! My guess is he struggled in the Me marriage mode more often than not.

Competition often occurs in Me marriage relationships. We are so caught up in our need to be right or superior that the goal of unity is forgotten. Unity in a marriage is unattainable as long as selfishness is the driving force. Most people don't realize how selfish they are. They are so conditioned by their family, cultural issues, or career training to meet their own needs, that they believe competition is a universal reality. In marriage, the only way two can stand up to all the challenges that will come, is if they work together.

Me marriage couples are defeated by these fears and rarely enjoy the benefits of a healthier relationship without making significant changes. The image of a red stoplight can remind you to take notice. If you are stuck in this style, stop what you are doing. The red light marriage is a warning that continuing down this path will be dangerous. Have you heard the saying that insanity is doing the same thing over and over expecting a different result? When you continue doing what doesn't work, the result is going to be the same. Regardless of how stuck you are, you can break the cycle by overcoming your fear. The power we give or don't give to fear will determine its impact. There are many obstacles to eliminating fear from your life. But with clear goals, faithful actions, and forward thinking, it can be accomplished. 1 John 4:18 proclaims, "There is no fear in love, but perfect love drives out fear, because fear has to do with punishment. The one who fears is not made perfect in love."

This book will discuss theories, skills, and examples of how to live in unity with your spouse, thus building the marriage of your dreams. As you work together, you will find that with solid skills, keen understanding, and the love of Christ, you can find the pathway to drive away fears.

"The goal of our life should not be to find joy in marriage, but to bring more love and truth into the world. We marry to assist each other in this task." —*Leo Tolstoy*

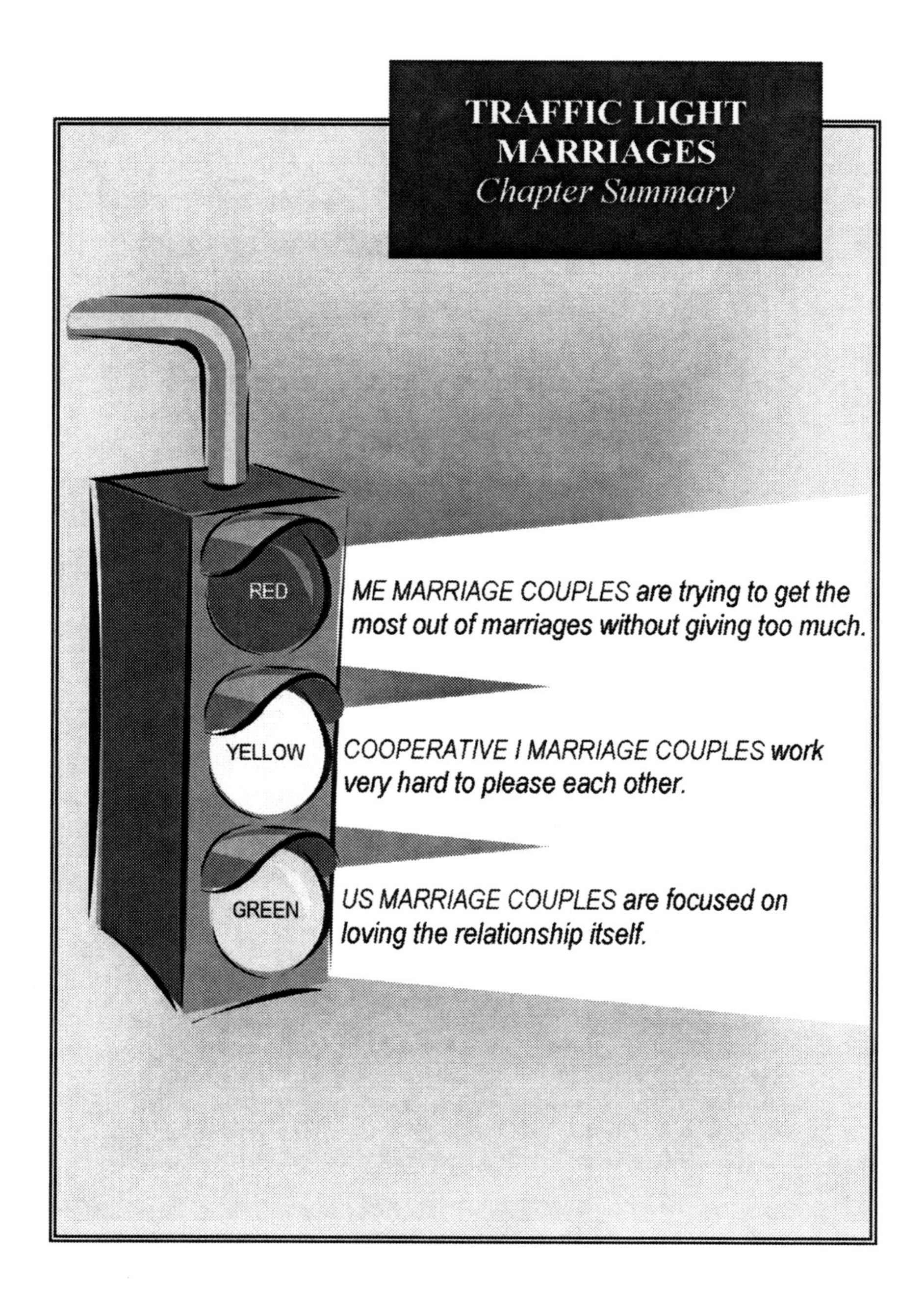
TRAFFIC LIGHT MARRIAGES
Chapter Summary
RED
ME MARRIAGE COUPLES are trying to get the most out of marriages without giving too much.
YELLOW
COOPERATIVE I MARRIAGE COUPLES work very hard to please each other.
GREEN
US MARRIAGE COUPLES are focused on loving the relationship itself.

*Section 2*

# The "5-C" Skills for Marriage

After working with hundreds of couples, attending numerous workshops, and reading dozens of marriage books, I am convinced that there are similar themes in all marriage relationships.

I refined my work with couples to design tools to assist couples in their marriage journey. In this section, I condensed my findings into five general tasks. They are: Compatibility, Communication, Cooperation, Commitment, and Closeness. I use the word *tasks* because it refers to the work in the marriage relationship. The five Cs should be on every successful marriage checklist. They are not always exciting, fun, or fulfilling until they are carved into productivity. Further, some tasks will take more effort to accomplish than others, while some will show up in the relationship more readily. Couples who master these tasks hit fewer snags, managing everyday struggles while on their way to enjoying a lifelong, fulfilling relationship.

Like building a home, there are certain steps or tasks that must occur to build a marriage. While there are optional features to be added in a home such as a fireplace, patio, or three-car garage, all builders include a foundation, windows, and a roof. In the same way, all marriages need a strong foundation to sustain the relationship.

The five Cs are those footings. Optional features such as career choices, type of cars you drive, and churches you attend can be decided later.

As you read about these tasks, imagine how your marriage would look if you were not completing any of these. If your marriage is suffering, reflect on which of the tasks need attention. I recommend you read each chapter carefully and then plan a course of action to remedy each problem you uncover.

*Chapter Two*

# The Collage of Compatibility

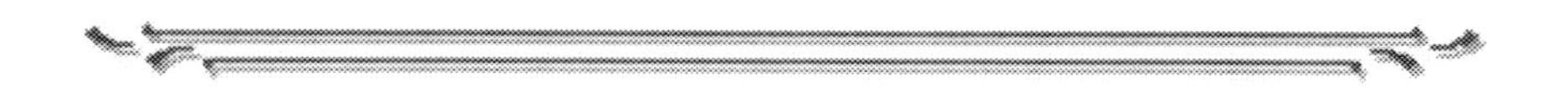

While working a puzzle one day with my two children, I realized that people often try to make their marriages work like a puzzle. Couple compatibility isn't like snapping two pieces of a puzzle together. Because of our vast differences and various origins, I find it amazing that any two people are ever compatible.

Webster defines compatibility as, "capable of existing together in harmony." As the kids and I struggled to make puzzle pieces fit, I wondered how many individuals don't really fit together. Unlike puzzles, in marriages there are no perfect matches. Puzzles have a finite number of pieces. Each piece holds one place in the picture. Even as frustrating as some puzzles are, the pieces do end up fitting together. Relationships, on the other hand, are built by bringing together unlimited variables.

Can you imagine working a puzzle where the pieces change their colors and shapes at will? That's how it feels to work out compatibility issues in marriage. It reminds me of the time I tried to capture a specific goldfish for my daughter, from a pet store aquarium that was filled with dozens of them. Each time I made a move to dip the net, the fish darted in the opposite direction. I ended up just scooping one up and convincing her it was the one she wanted.

Sound familiar to you?

The puzzle approach to relationships is ineffective because you simply do not fit just right with any one person. As long as you continue forcing the fit, you are denying each other your unique place in life. Marriage is more like a collage than a puzzle. Your aim is to be the right person in the relationship so that your interactions create a compatible marriage.

In this chapter we'll discover how to exist together in harmony. To begin, we must strive to be the right person for the marriage, rather than expect the marriage to be right for us. Consider that being the right person in a relationship may give you the best chance for compatibility. Conversely, partners who want to make their mate adapt to their specific desires and needs will be disappointed with the result. In the book *Relationships*, Les and Leslie Parrott suggest, "If you try to have intimacy with another person before achieving a sense of identity on your own, all relationships become an attempt to complete yourself."[1] Your marriage is only as strong as you are whole.

Some people marry partly because their mate exhibits opposite traits they believe will somehow make themselves better. Consequently, couples find themselves living with someone they don't like, don't respect, and don't want to be with. You can't simply replace your missing parts by borrowing parts of another person as if they were accessories. The borrowing concept will work at first, but only if I need your accessories as much as you need mine.

Like a collage, a marriage brings diverse and overlapping characteristics together. When the picture is finished you don't see a clearly outlined image of two separate people. What you usually find is a theme, cast from interrelating parts. The theme of a specific marriage is as unique as a fingerprint and is discovered as each couple learns to place its differences in proper perspective. Learning how to layer and integrate differences is the challenge.

John Wooden, the UCLA basketball coach from the 1960s and 1970s, is known as one of the greatest college coaches ever. His teams won a record seven straight national championships. Wooden's philosophy was to recruit players with speed and then design his strategy around the talents of his existing players. Every year he had a different team so he would have to redesign annually. What would it be like if we applied this same philosophy to marriage? Wooden picked his favorite quality: speed, then he built on that. What was the quality that attracted you to your spouse?

Designing your relationship around your favorite qualities could provide the same success Wooden found. Since marriages grow and change continuously, applying the Wooden approach to marriage gives power to the dynamically changing team. Forcing a mate's talents into a fixed game plan misses the true beauty of the team concept. The Us marriage is about building a new identity; one that draws from the talents of each person, yet has its own design and personality. If God is the central force in your marriage, allow Him to bring the collage together. It is my conviction that the spiritual connection is the only "relational glue" strong enough to hold this dynamic and matchless creation together. Our job is to let God, using our best qualities, design the relationship.

**The "3-A" Compatibility Formula**

The first step in the compatibility task is to understand how the personality is built. Personality includes three layers. The first is temperament, then attitudes and beliefs, and then expression, or overt personality. It's important to understand what part changes and what remains constant. The formula for working this out is:

*Acceptance*

Identify what cannot be changed about you and your partner and accept them as they are. (Basic Temperament Analysis)

*Alignment*

Explore your personal beliefs and work to gain insight, understanding, and respect for each other's beliefs and attitudes. This only happens when communication is safe, free of judgment, and authentic. (Beliefs Analysis)

*Adjustment*

Adjust to each other's unique style of expressing your beliefs.

Personality is just the voice-piece for personal beliefs. Each of you expresses yourself differently. Take the time to adjust to your mate's personality. Spend more time working on beliefs alignment. (Personality Analysis)

Temperament provides your basic floor plan or structure. Beliefs and values shape the person you are. Then, your personality expresses your temperament and beliefs. Your unique personality is served by your belief system. For instance, shy people can become public speakers and socially competent. If they believe they can learn how to overcome their shyness, their personality will accommodate that desire. Understanding how each partner interprets life will allow them to honor their differences rather than dispute them.

Note that personality remains stable, but belief systems can change. When beliefs are exposed and understood, then adjusting to another's style of expressing those beliefs is manageable. Behaviors serve beliefs and personality. That's why when you do something out of character your partner asks, "Have you lost your mind?"

***Acceptance of Temperament***

Being able to accept your partner as he or she is, is important to establishing workable compatibility. I am not suggesting you accept comments like, "I was not born to do laundry," or, "All women talk on the phone a lot." I am suggesting you discover your and your partner's God-given traits and count on them being constant. They will not change because you don't like them. Whether you like it or not, there is strong evidence supporting the idea that temperament is inherent. Genetic coding is responsible for eye color, hair patterns, and gender. It makes sense that genes contribute to personality development as well.

When my daughter was born two years after my son, I was convinced that we are born with "a style." While Seth hardly made a peep, Megan came to us with trumpets-a-blowin'. Ten years later, I can testify that same theme continues. Seth is a private person, preferring to retreat to the landscapes of his mind. He enjoys reading and interacting with electronics. Megan, on the other hand, creates a new landscape wherever she is. She is social and interactive with anyone who will give her an audience.

The critical issue in understanding these characteristics is that they are inherent. Changing basic temperament is no more possible than attempting to be six feet tall when you've been five feet tall your whole adult life. When you understand your temperament is unchangeable, you are better prepared to have patience with differences. Start today by simply accepting those aspects of yourself.

I notice in my own marriage that Jana and I take care of our clothes differently—she hangs hers up and I leave them on the floor! You may think this is learned but I have tried to keep my closet like hers, and for me, it is like trying to nail Jell-O to a tree. There is something inborn about the way she takes care of her things. I verify this reality every time I visit my in-laws. Her father's closet looks similar to what I see in her closet. I am not sure, but I don't think he had closet training exercises during her childhood. I also verify it when I visit my sister's house. Her closet looks very similar to mine. There are many behaviors that we can change to improve our lives. However, behind those decisions to change are God-given, deeply imbedded, uniquely made tendencies that last forever.

Ted Millon is one of my favorite personality theorists. He believes that three opposing motivators support personality development. The three polarities, or opposite tendencies, shape how we typically behave. The polarities are pain–pleasure, active–passive, and self–others.

The first set of opposites raises the question: Are we more motivated to *avoid pain* or *increase pleasure*? If you tend to avoid pain, you will behave very differently than if you are looking to increase pleasure. If you are at a party, are you the one who tells the jokes or the one who laughs at them but would never risk telling one?

The second polarity involves the question: Are we active about how we engage in life or do we allow life to come to us and maintain a passive approach to things? Some people are naturally more active in solving problems and taking charge of their lives. Others are observers of life and prefer to respond in a less dramatic manner.

The third polarity asks the question: Are we more oriented toward self or internal processing or do we reach out to others to solve problems and share thoughts? This is evident in how you are socially. If you are prone to be alone or have one or two friends, then you are more self-focused. If you are always around people and prefer to be with them to being alone, you are more others-focused.

These opposing motivators are ways to quickly identify what your basic temperament is. The combinations and degree of intensity of the three polarities are going to be different for both of you. Again, finding ways to accept those differences is the basis for good compatibility.

Gender differences are also evidence of inherited shaping factors. I am hesitant to speak to this issue because there are so many differing opinions. The popular book, *Men Are from Mars, Women Are from Venus*, and similar books published since, have torn down the walls between the sexes and provided insight into gender. Like all insight, however, when the lights are on but no one is home, what good is it? In my fifteen years as a therapist, I have found one thing to be true: insight alone does not produce change. You have to navigate your way through the differences found in your relationship. The red light or Me marriage type stems from what I referred to as our basic need to be the same. We struggle for acceptance. In doing so, we inadvertently diminish our uniqueness.

Compare a baseball to a soccer ball. They are both round, used for a sport, and can be thrown. That is their common ground. Conversely, one is hit and the other is kicked. One is caught with a mitt, while the other is caught bare-handed. A baseball is five times smaller than a soccer ball.

With gender, there is common ground, but also vast differences. Like rules for sports, men and women are raised with different rules. Men are taught to control their feelings; women are encouraged to express them. Little girls are dressed in pink and boys are dressed in blue. When a man and a woman get married, they agree to start playing "the game of life" together. In some ways, this is like a softball player trying to join a soccer game without knowing the rules. The softball player steps onto the soccer field with his bat and glove. When the ball starts rolling, his first reaction is to follow his instincts. He may start hitting the ball with the bat. He may attempt to catch the ball with his mitt. Imagine the chaos. He would be penalized often and booed off the field. This is what it feels like when men and women step on the marriage field. We forget our partners were trained differently. Our common ground can be deceiving. Don't assume your partner knows all the rules of the game.

As a married couple you are on an adventure. There are no rules until you establish them together! While most people begin playing with the rules they learned from observing marriage during childhood, it's an open playing field in each new marriage.

To help you on your adventure, I have listed some gender specific tendencies. Remember these are just gender generalities. If you don't fit the typical pattern I've outlined, that's okay. Ask yourself, If the statement doesn't fit you, does it fit most men or women you know? Use and discuss these at your own risk. No "Life-Guard" (relationship guard) is on duty!

### Top Ten Gender-Specific Tendencies

Men deal in facts, women attend to feelings
Men like accomplishments, women like experiences
Men under stress isolate, women under stress talk more
Men like electronics, women like beautiful things
Men ask for what they want, women ask what others want
Women are collaborators, men are competitors
Women enjoy dancing, men enjoy watching
Women like romance, men like physical touch
Women like smiles, men like wiggles
Women like security, men like structure

### *Alignment of Beliefs*

For effective compatibility in marriage, couples beliefs need to be in alignment. When your car steering is out of alignment, you struggle to drive because the car wants to pull to the right or left. This sensation is similar to couples who have beliefs that are heading in opposite directions. Like driving the car, the relationship is a struggle to maintain when beliefs are not guiding you in similar ways. The beliefs of each partner act as guidance systems for their activity.

For the most part, your belief determines how you feel and then act. When your thoughts are positive, your feelings are typically positive. When your thoughts are negative, your feelings are usually negative. The power of one thought can shape a destiny. If you think you are stupid, won't you feel stupid? Your thinking patterns are based on your belief system. Thoughts and observations of the world around you cluster to make up your beliefs. Consequently, how you choose to think is your most powerful tool for achieving personal success and fulfillment. The power to choose is often taken for granted.

In psychology circles, the power to choose is discussed by phenomenological theorists. They maintain that everyone has a unique way of interpreting events. I refer to this as perception interpretation. When a stimulus is detected by your senses, you have a moment of choice as to how you interpret that stimulus. How you perceive what is happening to you is partly determined by thinking about it. Boiling water is known to be hot, yet the degree of toleration for hot water varies. Some people like loud music because it symbolizes power or excitement to them. Others think loud music gives them a headache.

The power to choose how you think is your greatest mental asset. Unfortunately, because thinking is such a powerful tool, you can also sabotage yourself. The apostle Paul wrote a letter of instruction to the Philippians about this powerful force: "Finally brothers, whatever is true, whatever is noble, whatever is right, whatever is pure, whatever is lovely, whatever is admirable—if anything is excellent or praiseworthy—think of such things. Whatever you have learned or received or heard from me, or seen in me—put into practice. And the God of peace will be with you." When your thoughts are focused on constructive images, they will insure a belief system that will serve you in feeling good about yourself, others, and the world.

You carry many beliefs that do not serve you well, yet you hold onto them. For example, Frank thinks he is unattractive. That belief has shaped his opinion of women. He concluded that his personal value is based on getting the attention of beautiful women. His wife could never fully feed this hunger, so he seeks other ways to support his need for attention. When he is around beautiful women, he feels good. When they ignore him, he feels bad. This belief was the root of a sex addiction, poor self-esteem, marital failure, and numerous job losses. The power of his belief dominated both his internal and external world. Although he knows he feels this way, he doesn't realize he is bound by a belief that has never served him well.

What is the payoff of keeping a destructive belief? Can a belief change? The answer depends on the strength, meaning, and conviction of the belief. When I entered graduate school, I believed I was smart. As I finished my last year, I began thinking I was dumb. (Four years of graduate school has that effect on a lot of folks.) After surviving that gauntlet, I realized I had let graduate school pressure steal some of my positive self-image. Seeing how it could adversely impact my whole career as a psychologist, I let that negative belief go. Over time I had to relearn confidence in myself as a capable and intelligent man.

Frank can change his belief by replacing his neurotic need with a real need. He used his negative belief as an excuse to continue his addiction. If he wishes to end his addiction, he is free to change his perception of himself, thus allowing the belief to change. This type of addiction is not easy to change and often requires the help of a professional. Nevertheless, he is changing his core belief, which is dramatically improving his self-image. His wife can detect the difference in how he approaches and responds to her needs.

Our beliefs are only interpretations of events. We have the power to change our interpretation whenever we choose. It is not what happens to you that matters, it is how you react to what happens that counts. Couples can dramatically improve compatibility if they embrace this concept.

One couple I coach was able to use the "power to choose" technique to eliminate nagging and bickering. I convinced the wife she no longer needed to nag her husband about his household duties; she believed if he didn't complete his responsibilities it was her duty to inform him. I challenged that belief, asking her if she was pleased with the results of nagging her husband. She was not pleased, so I invited her to think differently about it. She informed me a few days later that she decided not to nag her husband anymore. She now believed that by nagging him, he would not take responsibility for his duties. This was not what she desired, so she was going to stop enabling him. Her belief was producing negative results for her. Even if he didn't improve his behavior, she would no longer be his scapegoat.

### *Adjusting to Personality*

Temperament is to personality what the chassis and engine are to a car. The performance you get from driving your car is based on the engine and mechanical parts. The way your car looks to others is based on the design and presentation. Your partner's temperament is what you would find "under the hood." Their personality is the way they decide to express or show those things on the inside. The idea of adjusting yourself to another person is easy for some and difficult for others. It requires a sort of resignation of being right for the sake of being compatible. When I think of adjusting to something or someone, I am reminded, for example, of having to respond to the weather changes that happen in Chicago. In the Midwest, weather changes are as unpredictable as watching a rubber ball bounce around a room. Like coping with weather, you and your partner are going to express yourselves in ways that require the recipient to constantly shift and adjust. Your personality, as well as your mate's, is the primary way you have learned to express your beliefs and feelings.

There are many influences that shape your personality. My doctoral training in the field of psychology was based on Adlerian Theory. Alfred Adler was a psychiatrist who worked with Freud and Jung in the early 1900s. They shared ideas and debated theories regularly. Unlike Freud and Jung, Adler was convinced people are not driven by instinct but rather by goals. He believed people develop a *law of unique movement* that serves as the template for how they interact with their environment. He called this *lifestyle*. We each have a personal lifestyle that guides our actions, thoughts, and dreams.

Lifestyle is shaped by early childhood beliefs, gender, and temperament. As mentioned earlier, temperament includes inherent traits acquired at birth. Temperament is fixed; we have to acknowledge it and accept it. The beliefs we develop in childhood, however, do not have to hold any basis in reality or make any sense. In fact, childhood is filled with nonsense stories, and it is common for children to develop real beliefs based on nonsense. They are simply beliefs we collect while struggling to understand our place in the world.

I have always found personality to be a fascinating subject. Personality is based on the way in which we express, interpret, and value our experiences. If one hundred people are watching fireworks, some will be impressed, others will be excited, others will be bored, and at least a few will be wondering who's going to clean up the mess when it's all over. These varied responses are the inevitable results of each individual's background, perceptions, needs, and fears.

Think of this "lifestyle" identity as the lens through which you view the world. I personally wear glasses to correct astigmatism in both eyes. Astigmatism is a vision problem caused by a deformity in the shape of my eyes and it leaves me viewing things slightly out of focus. Those who have tried on my glasses are always amazed at how "blind" I am. My personality is like my glasses. No one will ever know what life looks like through my filters. Through imagination, they can try on my personality type, but they can't see it the way I do.

No matter how hard you try, you will never see things as your partner does. The goal of a compatible couple is to value each other enough to remain curious and open to a different worldview. Being compatible is not about blending personalities. It is about respecting, valuing, and enjoying shared personalities that both partners bring to the relationship.

There have been numerous attempts to classify personalities. Psychologists are trained to assess personality based on maladaptive patterns. Extensive research has developed several useful measuring tools. The shortcoming to personality assessments is that they produce labels. While these inventories and tests are designed to give clarity and insight into who we are, they are not meant to define us.

For married couples, I recommend the personality inventories that Gary Smalley and John Trent published in their book *The Two Sides of Love*.[2] They took an age-old four-quadrant model and made it user-friendly. This tool suggests that people fall into one of four different quadrants or styles. While you may have many strong traits, one dominant or natural style stands out. The first of the four styles is Dominant. These people like to be in charge. They are born leaders and never back down from a challenge. The second is Fun. These people are the "life of the party." They enjoy life fully and believe everything in life should be fun. They look for ways to seek pleasure rather than to avoid pain. The third style is Relational. These people are warm, sensitive, and enjoy routines. They want emotionally secure environments. The last style is Analytical. Analytical people focus on precision and enjoy excellence. They seek relationships that derive from exact, measurable expectations. They would rather avoid pain than seek pleasure.

One misconception of personality differences is the unfortunate assumptions each style has to endure from the other types who don't understand them. While some find the Dominants' style overbearing and unwelcome, others value them for their ability to lead a corporation to unparalleled success. Likewise, the Fun type may be annoying to their more serious coworkers, but they are always welcome at parties. The Relational type is often regarded as too fragile and verbose, yet, if you need a good friend, they are the best. The Analytical style is easily viewed as negative and cold, but they will assure that their buildings and bridges are properly built. All their calculations are accurate and fair. Finding balance in your style, avoiding the tendency to become extreme, and adjusting to your partner's style is the secret to using this knowledge.

When you're stressed, any style's strengths can become liabilities. Remember, as a couple you're working on a collage with some overlapping and unrelated pieces. The picture of your marriage is designed with various colors, patterns, and textures. By accepting each other's differences, you can stabilize your connection. Aligning your beliefs will provide a compass that will get you both headed in the same direction. Adjusting to each other's personality style will allow you to understand one another. Enjoy your differences and realize that God is designing the unique collage of your marriage.

"A great marriage is not when the 'perfect couple' comes together. It is when an imperfect couple learns to enjoy their differences." —*Dave Meurer,* Daze of Our Wives

THE COLLAGE OF
COMPATABILITY
Chapter Summary
RED
If you marry the right person, they will know and understand you.
YELLOW
Work hard to be the right person for your partner.
GREEN
Strive to be the right person for your marriage, rather than expect your partner to be right for you.

*Chapter Three*

# Courageous Conversation

*While attending a marriage seminar on communication, John and his wife Lilly listened to the speaker declare, "It is essential that husbands and wives know the things that are important to each other." He addressed the men, "Can you describe your wife's favorite flower?" Tom leaned over, touched his wife's arm gently, and whispered, "Pillsbury All-Purpose, isn't it?"*

I have listened to hundreds of conversations between husbands and wives. Men and women alike struggle to get their point of view understood by their mate. Men are misunderstood as often as women are. The challenge of communicating effectively requires patience, like that of a mother helping her child tie his own shoes for the first time.

Sociologists tell us that early humans were able to manage all primary survival functions through body language: motions, gestures, and grunts. Oddly, this is still true. Research tells us that words make up only 7 percent of our communication. Verbal tones make up 38 percent of communication, and nonverbal language makes up the remaining 55 percent. If a couple wants to be effective at communication, they will want to be familiar and skilled at sending and receiving all three methods.

Communication is one of the five marital tasks in which

effectiveness is not negotiable. The quality of communication is the most familiar antagonist of marriage relationships. No other issue gets more press than this critical area of relationship success.

I've counseled people who are good at one method or another, but rarely find them effective in all three. You've probably met people who say the right thing, but their expressions don't match their words. Or you know a person who speaks clearly, but his voice is distracting. Nonverbal language has been researched and discussed for years. Can you imagine President Nixon without his two-finger wave? What we say, how we say it, and the nonverbal signals we send all play a vital part in sending and receiving messages.

Obviously, more talk doesn't necessarily make a better marriage. Effective communication often occurs more creatively without words. According to the aforementioned statistics, words have a minor impact on most communication—just developing a larger vocabulary might not impact our communication skills. Like driving a car without road signs or laws, using words without other communication skills will just add to the chaos. *Kahlil Gibran* wrote, "There are those who talk, and without knowledge or forethought reveal a truth which they themselves do not understand. And there are those who have the truth within them, but they tell it not in words."[1]

**Verbal Communication**

Still, words are a primary way couples demonstrate their interest in one another. Partners who know how they feel and what they think, and can articulate that awareness, are effective communicators. However, most couples don't feel only one way or think only one thing at a time and often have trouble articulating as changes occur. This can put a lot of stress on a marriage. Perhaps the most important tip for being an effective communicator is becoming clear about what you think and feel. To be blunt, don't speak until you know what you want to say and how to say it. James 1:19 makes a point with, "Everyone should be quick to listen, slow to speak and slow to anger, for man's anger does not bring about the righteous life."

My observation of marital dialogue leads me to conclude that most conversations are full of what linguists call "indirect communication." Defensive phrases, excuses, and revenge tactics are prevalent. Often judgment, generalization, and assumption are favored over empathy, clarification, and encouragement. Consequently, conversations may lack authentic interaction. Noel and Jan, the couple that helped me develop the Blue Ribbon Game mentioned earlier spent most of their time arguing assumptions. A dialogue may go like this, "He doesn't care about me at all. When he gets home, all he cares about is eating and watching television." He replies, "I don't talk to her because I know she will go on and on about how much she hates her work." This exchange could go on for hours without any empathic listening or straightforward questions, such as, "Why don't you talk to me when you get home?" Many couples find themselves stuck in this communication trap. It is a struggle to resolve the cycle. It reminds me of a man who said, "My wife says I never listen to her. At least I think that's what she said."

A powerful technique to penetrate the walls erected by this circular hypothesizing is called *leading with empathy*. Whenever you get stuck in this dialogue rut, try leading with empathy. The conversation might go better if Noel could respond to Jan with, "It sounds like you're frustrated with me for ignoring you when I come home." Then Jan could answer with, "I can understand that hearing me gripe about work is annoying and boring, but I need to sound off and I'd like you to be the one to listen." This empathic interaction is a step in the right direction to help Noel and Jan get back on track with their communication. Leading with empathy can quickly move the conversation to a productive exchange.

### *The Four Germs*

When communicating with your partner, words can take on various meanings depending on the state of your relationship. A wife asks her husband a simple question like, "Did you take out the garbage this morning?" If the husband is content in his relationship, he may simply answer yes without a second thought. If, however, the husband is feeling nagged or stressed about his marriage, he may read more into that simple question than what the mere words ask. He may then respond by saying, "Why, what's it to you?" The conversation will most likely lead to an argument about role inequities. When the relationship is infected with misunderstandings from past conversations, you may experience awkwardness in simple everyday questions.

John Gottman, in his book *The Seven Principles of Making Marriage Work,* named key damaging communication patterns the Four Horsemen.[2] He claims that these four horsemen charge into marriages in this order: criticism, contempt, defensiveness, and stonewalling. He predicts a marriage is doomed to fail when these four patterns are constantly present and the couple makes no effort to resolve them. While Gottman uses the horsemen image, I like to think of these patterns as germs. When a germ penetrates its victim, the victim becomes infected. Infections cause rampant breakdown in the whole system. Anytime words are spoken, these four germs seek to infect the conversation. It's human nature to dispatch these forces. They are readily available, powerful soldiers that require little maintenance.

*Criticism*

Most marriages include moaning and groaning over the duties and drudgeries of married life. This friction can either create tension or provide a path to effectiveness. The words that generate tension are usually laced with criticism. "I can't believe you made another mistake in our checking account! For a person with an accounting degree, you sure are stupid." Calling each other names and attacking personal character are both forms of paralyzing criticism. They leave a partner feeling defensive and discouraged.

Conversely, a grievance toward your partner would look and feel very different. "I am disappointed that you didn't get the trash out on time because I thought we agreed you would handle that task." This clearly identifies an emotion owned by the speaker and explains why it's there. In this case, the receiver better understands what actually disappointed their partner. They have a choice to correct the problem or discuss it further. Without a critical personal attack there is no need for defensiveness. A grievance is very different from criticism.

*Contempt*

This germ is more powerful than criticism because contempt implies a lack of respect. When respect is lost between partners, conversation can become a battle. Sarcasm, sneering, and hostile humor are all forms of contempt. Comments like, "You think you're God's gift to selling, don't you? If those idiots only knew what I know about you, they'd fire you," or, "I'm sick and tired of putting up with your excuses. Are you running for couch potato of the year?" can be damaging to developing the Us. When the germ of contempt penetrates a marriage, it cracks the foundation of solid love. Excuses for this unacceptable behavior range from "It's just my personality" to "She knows I don't really mean it." Yet, behind such negative comments is a person who has developed a deep disdain for the other partner. Without open and honest communication, this germ can kill a marriage.

*Defensiveness*

In sports, we hear "the best offense is a strong defense." Having healthy boundaries is a positive quality in marriage. Unfortunately, couples tend to forget that if they already love and respect each other, they don't need to be on the defensive. When defensiveness sets in, the couple loses the ability to resolve differences. Defensive people are usually insecure. Rather than expose their concern openly, they attempt to preserve an inflated image of themselves. A conversation I hear often goes like this:

*Wife:* It bothers me that you look at pornography.
*Husband:* Do you think I am some kind of pervert or something?
*Wife:* I'm just telling you it makes me uncomfortable.
*Husband:* I am not having affairs with those women. They mean nothing to me.
*Wife:* I wish you wouldn't look at them anymore.
*Husband:* I can't believe you think I'm a pervert.

This conversation won't resolve itself until the husband stops defending his image. Defensiveness is very difficult to work with and it eventually leads to callousness. Most people won't continue to discuss their feelings with a defensive person. They eventually shut down.

*Stonewalling*

When all three of the above germs are present for some time, a feeling of defeat may come over one partner. Stonewalling is a sign of hopelessness. Imagine the wife who attacks her husband with these poor communication methods the minute he comes in the door. He weakly attempts a defense and then leaves the room. Soon, he starts coming home later. He finds distractions to keep him away from the confrontations. He begins to avoid any conversation. His behavior incites her need to engage him. She screams louder and starts throwing things. He looks at her as if to say, "You're not worth my breath to speak," and continues to ignore her. We often call this the "silent treatment," and this can continue for days and weeks. Not talking to her punishes her more than yelling back. Some men would say they don't avoid their wives to punish them; they just want to avoid the hassle. Sadly, it all leads to the same outcome. Where there is no communication, there is no relationship. This communication germ is more prevalent among veteran couples. It takes time to build up the negativity and resentment that leads to stonewalling.

These four germs are not only contagious, but deadly. When you identify one or more of them, stop your conversation. Continuing a germ-infected conversation will inevitably end poorly. You are better off cutting your losses and trying again later.

***Tone of Voice***

The communication experts call tone of voice "paralanguage." Paralanguage considers the vocal component of speech apart from words. For example, consider this statement and how many ways it could be spoken: "Are you ready?" You may hear these three words in preparing for an exam, starting a race, or leaving on a trip. How do you respond? You respond according to the tone of the question.

We all know that tone can powerfully impact a conversation. Instead of confronting the tone, we often respond to the words.

This leads to confusion and arguments. The words "I love you" look good on paper, but can sound very different in tone. Both spouses say it before leaving each other for the day. Your wife could mean "I love you, have a great day, see you this evening." You could mean "I love you because I have to say it, and I hope you don't make me say it again tonight." This kind of paralanguage communication can go on for days, without the husband realizing the impact his tone is having on his wife. She may even ask him if he really loves her, and he may reply, "I said so, didn't I?" She "hears" the message he is really sending her, while he remains unaware of the building resentment. Sometimes we think we are hiding our feelings, but our tone of voice will usually reveal the truth.

In the book *Messages*, there are five different elements of paralanguage. They are resonance, articulation, tempo, volume, and rhythm.[3]

*Elements of Paralanguage*

| | |
|---|---|
| *Resonance:* | The shape of vocal cords determines the richness or thinness of sounds. |
| *Articulation:* | How carefully you enunciate your words sends messages of precision or lightness to the situation. |
| *Tempo:* | The speed of your words reflects emotions and attitudes. |
| *Volume:* | How loudly or softly you speak reflects emotions and confidence. |
| *Rhythm:* | Determines which words are emphasized in a sentence. |

An aspect of paralanguage is attraction to another person's voice. The sound of a voice can be soothing, like the sound of a mother's voice singing to her baby. There are voice patterns and pitch that are appealing to me. My mother's voice is still very comforting. Several years ago I was attending my paternal grandmother's funeral. My mother had written a letter to her mother-in-law to read at the funeral service. I had my head down, contemplating the loss, when I heard my mother's voice reading her letter. My body began to calm and a peace came over me during a very emotional time. I don't remember what she said, but I clearly remember feeling safe.

My wife's voice is also very attractive. Her voice has sweet sounds and tones that calm my most intense fears. Sometimes, when I am having a bad day, just a phone call with her can redirect my thinking. I remember when I was having a difficult emotional day because my father was dying and I couldn't be with him. She began to encourage me with her words, but all I remember was her voice giving me the energy back to finish my day. I can't remember what either my mom or wife said during those times, but I will never forget the sweet sound of their voices.

Some tones are appealing; others are annoying. Think how the "007" James Bond character speaks in his movies. His smooth, confident style woos the women and intimidates the villains. It's not so much what he says, or who the actor is, but how he says it. Now, consider the annoying voice of Fran Drescher, star of *The Nanny.* She makes a living with her strident voice.

Everyone participates in paralanguage communication. The following simple modifiers can create an undertone of irritation and disapproval when used with a negative tone of voice.

## Verbal Modifiers

| | | | |
|---|---|---|---|
| *Certainly* | *Sure* | *Only* | *Just* |
| *Merely* | *Still* | *Naturally* | *Again* |
| *Now* | *Slightly* | *Supposedly* | *Lately* |

*Below, see how these modifiers are used to send uncomfortable messages.*

| Words | Message |
|---|---|
| It's *only* a game. | There is something wrong with you. You're taking this game too seriously. |
| You *sure* have been tired lately. | There is something wrong with you, or you're up to no good. |
| I was *just* being frank. | There is something wrong with you if you can't take my honesty. |
| *Naturally*, you'll want to come. | There is something wrong with you if you don't want to come. |
| Are you *still* here? | You shouldn't be here. |
| I was *merely* making a point. | There's something wrong with you if you can't see my point. |
| You *certainly* are quiet. | You're too quiet and it bugs me. |
| *Come on*, let's relax. | There's something wrong with you and and you're annoying me. |
| You tried your best, *I'm sure.* | I'm not sure you tried your best. |
| *Now* what do you want? | You ask for too much. You're trying my patience. |

These examples show how verbal modifiers can change the message. *Now go back and read the sentences in the left hand column without the words in italics.* The covert jabs and insults are gone.

Controlling the paralanguage message requires self-awareness as well as constraint. A quote from John Wayne illustrates this awareness: "Talk low, talk slow, and don't say too much."

### Nonverbal Communication

We often respond to these gestures with more passion than we do words.

Fifty-five percent of the messages we send during conversation are completely nonverbal. Eye-rolling, smiling, winking, hand gestures, and pats on the back are vivid nonverbal communicators.

Some linguists believe that the average person spends ten to eleven minutes per day in verbal communication. The rest of their social interaction throughout the day is nonverbal.

Wouldn't it be incredible if the nation's primary and secondary educational systems taught the basics of nonverbal communication right along with reading and spelling? There is power in communicating nonverbally. Those around you are affected, either positively or negatively, by how you choose to interact nonverbally. It only benefits you to be aware of the impact your nonverbal communication has.

Pulling up to a stop light one day, I came upon a car full of young girls. I noticed they were all putting on makeup and chatting. I looked right at one of them and smiled. They all became aware that I was observing their activity and starting giggling. When the light turned green, I pulled away and obviously never said a word. We shared this awkward and funny awareness because I was momentarily transported into their space. Situations like this happen daily; do we notice them? A smile as someone walks by your office, a hand gesture signaling a car to turn ahead of you, or a bear hug given to your child are all examples of nonverbal communication.

In marriage, a scene of a husband reading a newspaper while his wife talks is a common example. As she speaks, he grunts responses sufficient to meet his basic listening requirement. The upheld newspaper indicates his real feelings. When the wife acknowledges his disrespect, the man throws down the paper and spews out a few choice words about her interruption. The marriage relationship is fertile ground for misunderstanding and detachment.

You may become so relaxed with your mate that you forget the subtle messages you send when actually saying nothing.

I can live in our house for days without noticing my piles of clutter. I don't pick anything up. Consequently, I don't notice my wife's nonverbal cues of disappointment and frustration. Jana also sends messages as a car passenger. She will "inhale" loudly when she perceives danger, leaving me with my heart in my throat. What is she telling me with her tense body movements and gasps for air? I perceive she is telling me that I am a terrible and unsafe driver. She says she just can't prevent her reaction. Jana and I don't fight much, but when we do it's usually in the car. As a result, we talk about our reactions to each other's style and work to adjust to the new awareness. I am more tolerant of her involuntary response, and she is striving to trust my driving. (I think I have the easier job, my driving is a little suspect!)

Next is a list of nonverbal signals and their meanings, taken from *Messages*:[5]

## Non-verbal Signs

### Eye Contact

*Generally seen as very important to demonstrate caring and respect.*

-- Normal eye contact means communication is open.
-- Looking down often means rejection.
-- Avoiding eye contact suggests someone does not feel secure or included.
-- A stare can mean dislike.
-- Eyes rolled upward may be associated with disbelief.

### Proximity

*Generally seen as a way of communicating comfort or familiarity to the other person.*

-- *Intimate distance* - 6 to 18 inches: For lovers, close friends, and children.
-- *Personal distance* - 1.5 to 4 feet: This is keeping people at arm's length. Perfect for a party or social gathering.
--*Social distance* - 4 to 12 feet: This is a safe space to conduct business and more formal social gatherings. A husband and wife may use this space to watch TV or read.
-- *Public distance* - 12 to 20 feet: Usually used at informal gatherings such as teachers working with students or employers talking with employees.

### Body

*General non-verbal sign.*

-- Stiff body or "freezing up" tends to show a person is lying or scared.
-- Defensiveness is shown by folded arms, crossed legs, body turned away.
-- Posture, such as lying down, standing up, or slouching, suggests a degree of relaxation in communication.

### Hands

*Generally relate to what is going on in the mind.*

--Hands that scarcely move or rest gently at one's side, suggest a calm, confident and self-assured person.
--Limp or hanging hands can signify boredom, restlessness, or tiredness.
--Picking or biting shows tension.
--Hand held flat with palm outward usually symbolizes "I don't know."
--Hands that are quite active signal a jittery, nervous, or uneasy person.
--Clenched hands often signify tension and frustration, or even anger.

### Facial Expressions

*Generally seen as a very powerful non-verbal tool.*

-- Smile indicates happiness.
-- Frown suggests unhappiness.
-- Wink suggests flirtation or acknowledgment.
-- Raised eyebrows suggest excitement or contemplation.

Reflecting on your personal communication effectiveness, I am sure you have been the recipient of poor communication. When the message you are getting is different than what your partner states, confusion sets in and you both feel misunderstood. Authentic expression takes self-awareness and thoughtfulness.

"The greatest problem in communication is the illusion that it has been accomplished." —*George Bernard Shaw*

**The Antidote for the Four Germs**

When you get an infection, the preferred course of action is to find a remedy. I have prepared an antidote for each of the germs previously described. Each of the antidotes are common ingredients of communication, yet when used in a timely manner, they have healing properties.

***Encouragement***

Encouragement is always welcome. When we encourage others, we support them by valuing their needs, preferences and opinions. When the germ of criticism is present, what better antidote is there than encouragement? When you are feeling the oppressive heat of criticism in your home, try cooling things off with encouragement. Criticism holds the most subtle danger of the four germs. It often masks itself as "honesty" or "just my opinion," but it stabs like a dagger into the character of a person.

I teach parents the difference between encouragement and praise. I think this explanation is helpful for couples to practice, as well.

Many parents tend to use praise and punishment for their reinforcement system. I tell parents that using praise develops praise junkies; using punishment develops bitterness. Both produce powerlessness. If you think about it, praise is an external reinforcement. When you give praise, the child believes he is making *you* happy. As parents, do we want our children to learn to make us happy or learn to do what is right? Teaching them *how* to think, rather than *what* to think, will equip them for life without us. Praise is a dangerous method of reinforcement. I want my child to feel that his accomplishments are building self-confidence, not parent confidence. What happens when he doesn't do well? He will likely assume parental disappointment.

The first time I remember using encouragement over praise with my son was just after his first parent/teacher conference. I sat down on a little chair and listened to this educator say the most incredible things about *my* son. I was beaming from head to toe. I came out of that school floating like a cloud with a tear in my eye because I knew I had a "good one." As I drove home, I contemplated what to say to Seth when it hit me, this was *his* thing. So when I sat him down on the couch, I said to him, "Seth, you received a great report card from your teacher; were you pleased with that?" He replied, "Yep," then ran off to play in his room. I was stunned. He was experiencing this huge victory in his life and all he said was, "Yep." I then reflected with my wife what kind of pressure I might have put on him if I had gone into my rehearsed praise party. He might well have hopped on the endless treadmill of "parental expectation syndrome." He was fine with what he had done, and I had no business making a big deal of it because I was proud. So I just encouraged him to continue his efforts. Like Seth, many of us need to have someone whispering what we already know, but need to hear it to bring out the best in us. Husband and wife are in a perfect position to create a support system for each other that can defeat those moments when they feel powerless, negative, and cranky.

Encouragement is versatile, use it frequently. Just giving praise or compliments is not as powerful as encouragement. In your marriage, discover ways of building each other up from the inside out. Don't rely on shallow external reinforcements. Have confidence in your mate's potential and be happy for them because they are worth it, not because it makes you feel good.

***Empathy***

I have been telling couples for years to "Lead with Empathy." Surprisingly, many adults do not understand the meaning of the word. The best way to describe empathy is by comparing it to sympathy. Sympathy is about how you feel—I feel sorry for that homeless man. Empathy is about how someone else feels—I wonder what it's like to live in a shelter and not know where my next meal is coming from. Empathy's motto is: "Put yourself in his shoes."

Empathy is powerful when used properly. Daniel Goleman, author of *Emotional Intelligence,* calls empathy "the fundamental people skill."[4] Is empathy a skill or an inherent trait? I was asked this at a seminar recently and an excellent discussion ensued. Empathy, like listening, is a skill—it can be taught and developed. Some people think they don't possess the ability to listen with empathy. It's not manly. It's for the maternal types. Men especially are not trained to intuitive emotions, so they often feel disadvantaged in this area.

The skill of empathy is critical as it relates to the germ of contempt. When a partner is totally disgusted and has declared war by way of contempt, the other partner must disarm them. Empathy is an effective antidote for the infection of contempt. The way to soften a cold heart is to warm it up with patience and understanding.

John and Jane are arguing about parenting again. She thinks he's too harsh and strict, and he thinks she's too soft. He comes home from work to a messy house, the kids screaming, and Jane on the floor trying to appease her youngest child. John finds this frustrating and shouts at Jane about the chaos. Jane quickly recoils and starts picking up the mess. Later when they talk she tells him, "You have an anger problem and I will not let you hurt our children. Did you have a bad day at work or something?" He says, "How can you say that?! The house is a mess. The kids are out of control. What have you been doing all day?" She responds by accusing him, "You are obviously in denial. Your kids are so scared of you they won't even let you put them to bed." By the time they arrive at my office, the bitterness is so deep John is stonewalling. He hasn't spoken to Jane for three days.

Now let's replace Jane's defensiveness by leading with empathy. What might have happened if Jane responded with empathy to John's agitation when he walked in the house? Jane could say, "I understand you have been working hard all day. I can imagine you are wondering why it's so chaotic." Isn't it probable that John would respond more favorably to this approach? Empathy can disarm defensiveness.

Leading with empathy keeps the conversation open and safe. The practice of acknowledging a partner's thoughts and feelings naturally draws him closer. When conversations are warm and comfortable, the inevitable outcome is safety. Many couples tell me their primary fear in talking to their spouse about tense issues is emotional safety. Communication with your partner is only effective when both partners focus on understanding each other. When this doesn't occur, any one of the four germs can produce chaos within minutes. In John Gottman's work, he suggests there is a three-minute rule. Within three minutes he can tell if the conversation is going to turn out bad. He maintains that a harsh beginning consistently destroys communication within three minutes. Because there is never a positive outcome, he recommends couples back out of the discussion and try again later.[5]

***Forgiveness***

Defensiveness often partners with guilt. Guilt is a good emotion as long as it motivates us to correct or atone for bad behavior. Defensiveness is a low-budget fix to avoid the real work of correcting a mistake or bad habit. Like encouragement, forgiveness can smooth the way for partners to face their demons. I like to play golf. When I'm not with scratch players, we usually play with a mulligan— a chance to replace a poor shot without penalty. Every marriage should have a mulligan (or two) available for "bonehead" plays. The awareness that your mate forgives you is a cushion that allows you to live with confidence. Conversely, when everything you do is scrutinized and criticized, you become hesitant and insecure. Those feelings are fertile ground for defensiveness.

Forgiveness begins and ends with the forgiver. The process of forgiveness is not about the offender. Whether the offender is suitably sorry or deserving has nothing to do with the process. Forgiving is a deeply personal growth opportunity for the forgiver. Lewis Smedes, author of *The Art of Forgiving,* suggests the forgiver goes through three stages of forgiveness.[6] They are:

1. Rediscovering the humanity of the person who hurt us.
2. Surrendering our right to get even.
3. Revising our feelings toward the person we forgive.

These can be very intense issues. I spend hours with people who were wronged, abused, and terrorized to an unimaginable degree as well as taken advantage of. When I suggest they work on forgiveness, they stare at me in disbelief. I can't tell you why some people can walk through these stages and others cannot. I will testify that forgiveness immediately brings a decrease in pain and suffering.

Forgiveness is the only path to complete healing for the violated person because it breaks the bond formed by the abuse. Sometimes we need to forgive because our spouse lies to us or fails to keep promises. These are more common offenses yet can still get in the way of having a healthy relationship. In order to clearly explain this theory of forgiveness, I am choosing to use infidelity as a case study. Keep in mind the same process could be used for lesser offenses.

Forgiveness for infidelity is one of the most difficult challenges for married couples. The gut-wrenching suffering that occurs in the aftermath of infidelity is matchless. Since infidelity is often a symptom of an illness within the partnership, forgiving must begin with realizing the humanity of the offender. Keeping the focus on the partner rather than the pain can help. In doing this, betrayed partners may discover their role in the infidelity. A variety of issues, ranging from diminished attention to the Us all the way to sexual incompatibility, can lead to infidelity. Whatever the situation, you need to focus on your partner's humanity (meaning we are all human and are capable of doing harm to others) and view the behavior as separate from the person.

Couples who attain this first stage have to then purge all vengeance fantasies. It's human nature to want to even the score by going out and cheating on the offending mate. Obviously, this spells disaster and only leads to more pain and suffering. Perhaps the most common vengeance is to remain faithful, but to torture the offending mate with put-downs and probing questions about the details of the infidelity. This line of questioning is abusive to any relationship and drives both partners further from healing. Giving up the right to punish is the only healthy course of action.

Once partners have accomplished these first two stages, they can work unhindered toward recreating a secure relationship. Many people fear this most. They don't see themselves ever getting past the pain to feel secure with that person again. This is a normal part of recovery. Sometimes, trusting the process is all you can do when the feelings aren't there.

Understanding the concept of the marital Us during this time helps both partners sacrifice to save the relationship. Feeling good about the relationship is a baby step on the path to feeling good about the person. Contributions made to the Us relationship eventually pay dividends in the form of a new, joyful marriage raised up from the ashes of infidelity. If you are struggling with infidelity or other relationship violations, consider taking the steps necessary to forgive your offender.

***Listening***

The fourth gem—listening—counteracts stonewalling. Because stonewalling is nonverbal, you need to respond to it nonverbally. What causes this communication pattern is too much talk about the wrong things. The germ infects when a mate realizes that his or her input is disrespected or not heard. Upon discovering that they will not be heard, partners just tune out. Both partners must have their turn listening and speaking, to secure that their feelings and thoughts matter to the other person.

There are three levels of listening. The first level is *hearing*. When you hear information, you have the physical sensation of the incoming information. The second level is *fact-finding*. This level includes listening for information and remembering what was said. If you are listening at this level you can repeat back what the speaker said. You do not understand the message yet, but you can repeat it. Level three is *empathetic* listening. To understand the message you need to be at this level. You can hear, learn, and feel what the speaker has said.

Level 1: *Hearing*: Physical sensation of hearing, no learning.
Level 2: *Fact-finding*: Hearing and remembering what is said, without meaning.

Level 3: *Empathic*: Hearing, remembering, and feeling what is said.

Effective listening is a skill requiring effort. Once, during a listening workshop, a participant raised her hand to comment. "Listening requires a lot of concentration and I hate to say it, but it's something I have not been willing to do in most of my relationships."

Without effective listening, connections are disrupted. Jana and I were out with another couple recently. The husband had been unemployed for several months, and we were discussing his job search. He said people often called to inquire about his job search, but he quickly knew if their queries were genuine or not by how well they listened to his answers. Some would open the conversation with a question about his job search, but then turn the discussion to some story from their experience. The phone call would end with my friend uncertain if they called to support him or to get support from him. He found the experience unsettling and awkward. Listening requires one person's needs to be set aside.

Far too often, I have conversations with others where none of us truly hear or listen. Many short greetings throughout the day illustrate this struggle. While walking past someone in the hall, you might say, "Hey, how are you doing?" They say, "Fine, how are you?" Nothing else is said, and nothing else is required. Because of these superficial social interchanges, you may pass over someone who needs to talk. Or I ask someone if they are enjoying their job, and when they say, "No, because…" I tune them out. If they say, "Yes," then I'm out of the woods and on to another superficial subject. This sort of interaction happens to couples every day. They greet each other with a, "Hi, how are you?" Inside, they're thinking, "Please don't give me a long answer; I need to get dinner started and go through the mail."

Two effective listening techniques are based on the research of marriage and family organizations. The first is found in the book, *Fighting for Your Marriage*.[7] The second is Gary Smalley's interpretation called the "Drive-Through Talking" technique.[8] Each focuses heavily on the listening process.

The first one is the Floor technique. It is based on the premise that the speaker has the floor. While at a training workshop in Denver, I observed the trainers demonstrate this technique by actually using a piece of tile or carpet. The rule is whoever has the "floor" is the speaker and the other person listens. The speaker has to use "I" messages and brief comments, be mindful, and not ramble. The listener cannot speak until called upon to paraphrase the speaker. The speaker then affirms or denies that the paraphrase is correct and notifies the listener of what she missed. This process continues back and forth until the speaker is confident the listener understands him. The magic happens as the speaker becomes more concise and focused so the listener paraphrases correctly. When the process concludes, a message has been spoken, heard, and understood.

This single technique could save many marriages, if implemented properly. Couples who first do this exercise in my office or at seminars inevitably miss the message on the first attempt. Yet, with practice, when a person is heard and understood, productive conversation follows. As a youth pastor in the mid 1980s I used a similar technique. When the kids and I had group discussions and everyone began talking at once, I would pass around this silly stuffed toy. Whoever held the toy could speak, everyone else had to listen. We had many productive conversations as the toy was tossed around. The "floor" can serve your marriage in a similar way. Jana and I even have a "floor" magnet on our refrigerator to use during misunderstandings with our children.

Gary Smalley's "Drive-Through Talking" process comes from fast-food restaurant protocol. I relate to this because I'm the fast-food king. Imagine pulling up to a popular fast-food drive-through window, stopping at a speaker and menu board, and waiting. The attendant lets you know when he is ready to take your order. You say, "I want two double cheeseburgers—only mayo; two kid's meals—one chicken, one burger. With the kid's meals, I want a Hi-C and a Sprite. I also want two medium Diet Cokes." The attendant repeats the order, but the drinks are wrong. I repeat the part he missed. We go back and forth until we agree on the whole order. We then pull up and check to make sure the order was filled properly, much to the dismay of the folks behind us in line. When all goes well, everyone wins. We received the food we ordered, they get their money for the service. Now, many menu boards have a lighted digital printout of the order, to ensure correct translation.

The key to this technique is for couples to be willing and honest about what they need. It may go something like this: Husband says, "Welcome to listener's buffet, you order, I listen." Wife says, "Honey, I need you to remember to put your clothes in the basket after you wear them. I am trying to train the kids to do this, but when they see you don't do it, they don't do it either." He says, "Okay. You're saying if I don't start picking up my clothes after I wear them, I am a bad parent." She says, "No, I didn't say that. What I said is, I want you to pick up your clothes because it's good for the kids to see us acting consistently with what we teach them." He says, "All right, you want me to be more consistent with picking up my clothes, so I set a good example for the kids." She says, "Yes." He says, "I can do that."

Drive-Through Talking can save couples headaches by absorbing misunderstandings before they get too far out of control. Many times what you say the first time is not fully understood by your partner, and clarification is needed. I invite you to practice either of these similar methods. While the techniques may feel unnatural at first, if you hang in there you will develop a comfort and style that works.

For years I have observed communication between couples, and have received great satisfaction when I am able to assist them in being more authentic, clear, and effective. Remember that what you say to your spouse is heard more from nonverbal and tone of voice, than from the literal words you use. I recommend you follow up communication mistakes with the four communication antidotes; encouragement, empathy, forgiveness, and listening. If you use them, it will permanently, and significantly improve communication in your marriage. I passionately encourage you to make the skill of communication a high priority to practice and frequently develop.

"Words are just words and without heart they have no meaning."
—*Chinese proverb*

COURAGEOUS
CONVERSATION
Chapter Summary
RED
Keep to yourself, don't rock the boat.
YELLOW
The more you talk, the better.
GREEN
Words are essential, but can bore marriages to death if overused.

*Chapter Four*

# The Cooperation Challenge

In a district of Germany there was an old custom for testing whether a couple was suited for marriage. Prior to the wedding ceremony, the couple was taken to a clearing where a tree had been cut down. They were given a two-handed saw and asked to cut the trunk in half. This test quickly revealed how cooperative the couple was. If they did not trust each other, they would tend to tug at one another and accomplish very little. If one person dominated the other, even if the other person gave in willingly, the job would take twice as long. The secret to accomplishing the task was combining their efforts in a unified action.

I admire this custom because it illustrates that the whole community took marriage cooperation seriously. Just imagine if American marriages were built on this condition. Men and women would discover quickly how to work together as a couple. Cooperation doesn't come naturally. To fully enjoy the benefits of cooperation, the needs and desires of those wishing to be in a relationship must be expressed. I am defining cooperation as the mutual agreement to intentionally engage in activities together directed toward a common goal.

The social skill of cooperation is first introduced in the interaction between infant and caretaker. As the primary caretaker, for example, the mother begins to develop a working relationship with her child. In those early days, the caretaker is needed around the clock to hold, feed, and entertain on demand. Soon, however, a schedule is required for the baby to thrive as well as for the mom to survive! Then, the parent guides the child into a routine that teaches the baby the difference between 12 a.m. and 12 p.m. feedings. A wise mother will be predictable, so that the baby can come to expect and trust the schedule. In short, the child learns to cooperate with mom's routine. However, if the caretaker neglects structure in a child's life, responding to his every cry and whim, the child is not required to regulate anything but his own needs. We all know what happens when children like this grow up. Pampered children make difficult soulmates. They are reluctant to cooperate unless they believe their needs take priority. The best hope for them is to enter relationships that confront and reshape their self-focus.

Just as a flower needs sunshine, people need to belong. In the early 1900s, psychiatrist Alfred Adler realized this and described it as "social interest." The term *social interest* came from his observations of humans struggling to connect in social relationships. He studied how a person negotiates loyalty to community versus individual needs. Dreikurs, an apprentice of Adler, suggests, "Social interest depends on how soon he makes contact with others, whether and to what extent he can adapt himself to others, whether he is capable of feeling with and understanding other members. A man who only thinks of himself, of how he is to uphold his own dignity and the role he means to play, is sure to cause trouble within his circle of friends and acquaintances."[1]

Understanding social interest as a basic human longing can help create cooperative marriages. One resounding theme borne from the 9-11 tragedy was the move toward community. Cities pulled together, businesses raised funds, and people were united in love for their country. How can we capture that kind of "feeling" in marriages across the country?

The passion behind this book is based on my experience that couples have become too focused on meeting their individual needs to the neglect of their relationship. I invite you to embrace the notion that you and your spouse both desire connectedness. This desire can be fulfilled when cooperation is practiced in the marriage relationship.

Couples who merge into a cooperative spirit when facing conflict are more likely to survive their oppressor. We must learn to move together as we engage in our daily lives. Real joy transpires when transcending personal interests for the good of the relationship. Security, love, joy, and peace of mind all stem from each partner in a relationship surrendering itself to social interest. To help you develop more cooperation, I explain it with three practices that require steady development. They are friendship, fighting, and family.

**Friendship**

Most strong marriages begin with strong friendship. Cooperation in marriage is maintained by that friendship. Aristotle defined friendship as one soul abiding in two bodies. There is something pure and honest about a good friend. Friendship makes me think of three threads woven together that build a strong fabric. These are common interests, acceptance, and loyalty.

Falling in love does not equal good friendship. Let's use a simple illustration. If I buy a flashlight, I'd like it to have batteries. It needs batteries to work. More often than not, however, batteries are not included. Likewise, friendship doesn't automatically come with love. Nevertheless, friendship, like the battery, is needed to make love work. The friendship of a married couple provides the foundation for romance and passion. It is no surprise that these two essentials are often lacking in marriage relationships. Without the security of deep friendship, passion burns out.

"To be a friend to one's lover or members of one's family may seem odd to some, but is certainly a wise insight, for friendship brings with it a keen desire to know someone, the major requirement of love. It entails a healthy curiosity directed away from oneself—to others in an uncompetitive, non-exploitative, non-manipulative way.

It is an unselfish desire to experience other humans as they are and to draw them close enough to allow them to tell us safely who they are." —*Leo Buscaglia*[2]

***The Shared-interest Thread***

Having shared interests is a common denominator for all friendship. Shared activities and hobbies lay the groundwork for friendship to grow strong. Simply put, when a couple cooperates in a shared activity, their marriage is more likely to maintain closeness and vitality. Conversely, when one individual in a friendship no longer stays connected to a shared interest, the friendship experiences a rift.

Couples have to be wary of this occurrence. When the activities two people enjoy together become few and far between, the aspect of friendship becomes diffused. This often happens when children arrive. Be alert by taking the time to feed the friendship as routinely as you feed your children.

***The Acceptance Thread***

Acceptance in a friendship affirms the worth of both individuals and solidifies their connection. When my wife and I began dating in college, we both studied psychology, enjoyed similar activities, and spent lots of time together. Eventually, our friendship deepened and our relationship became serious. I felt a strong sense of being desired. When Jana agreed to marry me, I was amazed. Of all the men she could have picked, she chose me. (You will never know how cool that was!) The acceptance I felt was profound, increasing my confidence tenfold.

When couples choose to cooperate and accept each other for who they are, annoying differences, habits, and pet peeves become less significant. In daily life, both partners need to understand or overlook character flaws. Accepting one another is the foundation for building trust and safety. Author Nathaniel Brandon states, "When we fight a block it grows stronger. When we acknowledge, experience, and accept it, it begins to melt."[3] Couples will head off problems when they are unified by acceptance.

### *The Loyalty Thread*

Zebras can teach us a lesson in loyalty. When the herd senses a predator, they stop together and form a "caution circle." When their safety zone is violated, they all take off together. Their stripes make them easy to spot when standing alone; however, when running together their lines become blurred, making it difficult for predators to target just one. They instinctively move together, cooperating for the sake of their lives. How many times are we prone to move in our own direction when danger is present? Spouses who choose their own way and become disloyal to the partnership are prone to situational temptations like excess work, affairs, or addictions. Partners who join to form a "caution circle" during conflict are more likely to survive tenuous situations. Loyalty preserves the connection that two people have and provides marriage security.

I recall a Bible story about two very close friends named Jonathan and David. The book of I Samuel tells us that Jonathan's loyalty to his friend David was so strong he stood against his own father, King Saul, on his friend's behalf. Because David was a great leader and the people loved him, Saul jealously ordered David executed. Jonathan pleaded with his father to spare David's life. The loyalty, respect, and admiration these two friends shared saved David's life. As loyal spouses, it is our responsibility to stand up to those situations that would threaten our marriage. Loyalty is one tremendous quality of friendship. The faithfulness of a close friend is priceless.

### Fighting for Us

I occasionally have a "good laugh" with some couples returning to therapy after a few years when we discover they are still fighting over the same things. I asked one couple, "Whatever happened with that spare bedroom you were going to remodel?" They responded, "We haven't touched it because we're still arguing over the color of the carpet." This conflict presents a challenge even though resolution may not be necessary for the couple to continue in a productive marriage. This couple came back to therapy to adjust to their last child leaving home, but never brought up the spare room in conversation. John Gottman said, "Marriage is successful to the degree that the problems you choose are ones you can cope with."[4] Admitting that a conflict won't be resolved can save hours in unnecessary battle.

If you are unsure how to identify conflict before it becomes ugly, I encourage you to look for signs that one or both of you are avoiding something. Not all couples are screamers. Some couples are passive fighters, some are "wanna-be" fighters, and others fight like gladiators. Regardless of your style, you are probably in a relationship where one of four behaviors emerges when conflict is present. I call them the Agitating A's. These behaviors indicate resistance that may require conflict management skills. If you let the four agitating patterns continue too long they become imbedded and very difficult to manage.

***Apathy***

Apathy, the lack of concern or emotion, may be a silent contributor to marriage breakdowns. When a partner shares exciting news with the other and the response is apathetic, it can be deflating. If a request from one spouse is viewed as stupid or unnecessary, they are left feeling unworthy or unappreciated. Remember this is the love of your life, not the grocery clerk. Don't allow marriage to become stale. Stay alert and notice your spouse. Their feelings, thoughts, and experiences should be held in highest regard, even if you don't agree with them. Validate your partner's feelings before disclosing yours.

***Arguing***

When spouses cannot agree or compromise, arguing may occur. Arguing can be very destructive. After accumulating twenty years of research with couples, the authors of *Fighting for Your Marriage* maintain that escalation, invalidation, withdrawal and avoidance, and negative interpretations, are key indicators for relationship failure.[6] Arguing often triggers all four of them. The following story illustrates the four behaviors.

After a long day at work, Jane came home to find a terrible smell in the kitchen. She found out that the garbage had not been taken out again, even though she had left a note for her husband,

John, earlier that morning. She realized John was in the upper level of the house lying down. Because of the fire building up inside her, in a loud tone she burst out at the bottom of the stairs. "John, can't you read?" she yelled. "You know how leaving the smelly garbage around upsets me! I only asked you to do one thing and you couldn't even do it." John was upstairs taking a nap. After having a hard day at work, he awoke a little dazed by the whole situation. He then yelled back downstairs, "I never saw the note. Why didn't you put it somewhere I could see it? Besides, I didn't smell a thing when I came in. You're overreacting. What's the big deal?" John then turned over on the bed hoping the whole thing would just go away. Jane, so angry that she wasn't getting any respect, stomped over to the garbage and contemplated walking it upstairs to dump it on John's head. She then began to feel sorry for herself and took the garbage out. The rest of the evening, with the door locked, she watched TV in their spare bedroom.

*Escalation*: Sometimes before we have had a chance to find out what really happened, we respond to what we see, rather than finding out what really may have happened. John came home from work early feeling sick, took two aspirin, and thought he would take a little nap to see if that would help. Our response escalates and ends in disconnection.

*Invalidation*: John didn't consider Jane's feelings when responding to her sense of smell. Just because he didn't smell anything does not mean Jane is overreacting. When you don't acknowledge your partner's feelings, they will feel misunderstood and negated.

*Withdrawal and Avoidance*: Jane and John continued to avoid each other the rest of the night. This supercharged the feelings by not discussing them. It may be a few days before this couple talks about their experience and by then the damage is done.

*Negative Interpretations*: John and Jane negatively interpreted each other's comments. Jane was inconsiderate for assuming John read her note and didn't do what she wanted. John's negative reaction to Jane suggests that she doesn't know how to properly leave a note.

***Acquiescence***

"Pushover" and "doormat" are words that describe this agitating behavior. This response seems acceptable because there is the appearance of good in it. For some reason, yielding to your partner seems to make sound intuitive sense. Unfortunately, the person doing the yielding can be easily taken advantage of. Often, the yielding partner uses resentment as a weapon later. The end result tends to produce bitterness and too much power on one side.

In her marriage, a wife who yielded thought she was being the perfect mate. Her husband worked long hours, so instead of asking him for help with the kids, she raised them herself. He needed recreation to have an outlet for his stress, so he played golf two or three times a week. He needed friendship with other men, so he went on long golf weekends with his friends and was heralded by them for having such a great and understanding wife. She lived with the belief she was sacrificing for the good of the marriage and that her sacrifices would pay off. This pattern of yielding went on for twenty-six years until one day she realized her husband had a girlfriend. Suddenly, it all became clear to her. She yielded to avoid conflict, while he took her behavior as freedom to live an irresponsible life. She neglected her own needs so long that the marriage no longer required her presence. The devastating truth about acquiescence is that conflict is not avoided, it is perpetuated.

***Anger***

In the first three minutes of conversation, a trained therapist can determine if the balance of the conversation will be productive. When anger enters a conversation, hope dims for cooperation. Anger is a normal emotion that generates powerful surges in the body. When this eruption takes place, the only acceptable action is to step away from the situation and take time to cool off before continuing.

Everyone experiences anger at one time or another. You may be struggling with anger yourself or in a relationship where anger hinders communication. I grew up in a house where anger was unacceptable. My parents did not raise their voices and they did not permit screaming among the siblings. Consequently, I did not learn to identify or deal with the anger I experienced in others and in myself. This left me unprepared to deal with the unfortunate task of managing a powerful emotion. It is important to deal directly with anger to avoid lengthy entanglements.

### *Responses to Conflict*

Conflict generates a variety of physical, emotional, and mental responses. When we perceive a threat, our bodies flood with adrenalin for "fight or flight." Raised blood sugar levels, increased heart rate, and general edginess mark this emotional state. The body is armed for anything.

When we feel attacked, we are vulnerable to several emotional states. The connection between unresolved conflict and heightened emotional states can be exacerbated by stress. Research clearly shows that stress can make any potential problem worse. One problem attributed to stress is called flooding. Flooding occurs when emotions are experienced faster than the mind can process them. Flooding produces confusion and increased emotional outbursts. When this emotional state is experienced, conflict can be almost impossible to disarm except by distancing. Other less intense emotional reactions can be channeled to support the primary goal of the conflict. That goal needs to be specifically clarified before emotions can be useful.

For example, if you are fighting with your partner about keeping the house clean, the conflict will focus on the issue of housecleaning unless underlying issues are addressed. If there are unspoken issues, the fight may escalate as competence, fairness, and historical evaluations are introduced into the conversation. If you identify the real issues up front, communication can focus on finding solutions rather than bickering over vague emotionality. For best results, emotions should never guide a conflict.

To be sure, there are times we must agree to disagree. Our response to conflict will determine how effective and fulfilling our relationships can be. Conflicts can be addressed by using any number of conflict resolution techniques. I use the share technique. Use this method as a training ground for becoming better conflict managers. As a couple, you will eventually develop a personal style or template for dealing with conflict.

# SHARE

## Conflict Management

**S** Show mutual respect
**H** Hit the real issue
**A** Alternative brainstorming
**R** Reach an agreement
**E** Evaluate your progress

### *Show Mutual Respect*

Right or wrong, we each have our own point of view. When conflicts arise, it's helpful to demonstrate respect for our spouse's position. Otherwise, the best-case scenario is a win-lose arrangement. Mutual respect is not simply a positive attitude but rather an acknowledgement of our spouse's right to his/her perspective.

### *Hit the Real Issue*

More often than not, couples are not fighting over things like money or sex. We tend to be more concerned about the "WHO" questions. Who is right? Who is in control? Who will win? Who will decide? Who is important? This type of battle takes place in the backdrop of everyday struggles.

### *Alternative Brainstorming*

Once the real issue is identified, take a few moments to look for alternative ways to solve the problem. It is helpful to use possibility thinking to come up with creative alternatives. What is possible if we really wanted to resolve this? What are all the possible angles we could pursue? Make a list of 5-10 solution options. Most problems have at least 4-5 possible solutions.

### *Reach an Agreement*

Each partner examines what he/she is willing to do with no "strings" attached. *Suggestion:* It is helpful when reaching an agreement to consider what you are willing to do for a short period of time.

### *Evaluate Your Progress*

After reaching the agreement, decide to meet at a fixed time in the future to evaluate the outcome of the new decision. This will enable adjustments to be made, if needed, to ensure fairness between partners.

**Family**

We each have our own vision of belonging to a family. Holiday rituals, gatherings for weddings and funerals, and rallying because of disasters all reinforce our connectedness. When these experiences are less than ideal, and they often are, it's tempting to bash family ties and seek refuge in empty selfish pursuits. But no man is an island. We *are* connected, even when refusing to acknowledge it. Recognizing cooperation as a marriage task necessitates understanding the importance of family. Knowing who you are is as much about family awareness as self-awareness.

Family issues are consistently considered a leading cause for divorce and marital dissatisfaction. Wallerstein and Blakeslee consider the first undertaking of every married couple to be separation from their family of origin. According to the authors, "The first task in any first marriage is to separate psychologically from the family of origin and simultaneously create a new kind of connectedness with the parent's generation. These intertwined tasks, seemingly in opposition are mutually necessary."[5]

It's never easy defining boundaries and negotiating family relationships. Nobody gets married free of family issues. Many couples aren't even on good terms with their own families before marrying, let alone prepared to integrate with another family.

Each couple works their way through the process while forming a new marriage identity. The new identity is critical because it sets the tone for what form this new connectedness will take. No couple is an island, either. When parents and in-laws sense their adult child is being taken advantage of or badly treated, they often find it difficult to refrain from butting in. The strength of the couple's marriage determines to what extent these intrusions will damage the marriage. Each couple must cooperatively develop a plan to manage their parental relationships satisfactorily. This is often the first conflict couples face together, so teamwork is the key.

Couples who survive this transition will tell you they found balance when they began their own traditions and rituals. I can remember Christmas mornings with my family being fun and exciting because we always opened the gifts first thing in the morning. On the first Christmas with my wife's family, we opened the gifts on Christmas evening. I was so bummed! Who in their right mind does that? Well, as I learned over the years, many people do. When children arrived, Jana and I decided to have our own traditions, so we could share the new excitement together.

I also recommend honoring rituals in your relationship. These could be as simple as having coffee each morning, kissing before leaving for work, or squeezing butt cheeks at the same time while saying, "I can hold on till I see you again." Whatever they look like, sound like, or feel like, having rituals provides your relationship with a family characteristic. It is important to have your own rituals while personally continuing to enjoy those brought from your own family experience. Of course, this is only if you wish to keep them. Like an outdated tie, some would be better off forgotten.

In summary, marriage relationships face the three Fs for success in the cooperation task. Friendship builds a support structure for fighting to be productive. When fighting is productive, family relationships prosper. Identifying ways to master friendship, developing effective conflict skills, and enjoying family connections will greatly enhance cooperation in your marriage. This is an active juggling process throughout your marriage. I challenge you to become an excellent and joyous juggler.

"For marital happiness especially, observance of the rules of cooperation is imperative, since marriage is the closest kind of living together—the most intimate association between two human beings." —*Rudolf Driekurs*

THE COOPERATION CHALLENGE
Chapter Summary
RED
Take what you can get.
YELLOW
Compromise with each other to keep the peace.
GREEN
Neither person gets their own way. The relationship wins.

*Chapter Five*

# Commitment Capabilities

Twenty-two years ago, a powerful conversation with my father changed the course of my life. It was my senior year of high school and we were traveling to visit a college. As my father and I discussed my future, the topic of developing people came up. He shared his unrealized dream of becoming a psychologist, and we discussed what being a psychologist meant and how I could make a career of it.

This conversation was a pinnacle moment because that day I made a decision to go to college and study to become a psychologist. Not long after, I left Indiana to attend a small college in Illinois, committing to a course of schooling that would demand the next eleven years of my life. Finally, at the age of twenty-eight, I earned my doctorate in clinical psychology. Thanks in part to my relationship with my dad, I was able to accomplish a major goal. Although there were many obstacles, I was able to dream, start, and finish the objective.

I learned three compelling words from my high school basketball coach that served me well in pursuing my goal as a psychologist. Commitment is achieved by applying *desire*, *dedication*, and *determination* to every goal. I have invoked this 3-D tool often to assist me in achieving new goals. Finding creative ways to utilize this simple process has developed my capabilities toward commitment.

These three words can benefit couples aspiring to succeed at the long-term relationship called marriage. The great cathedrals of Europe often took a century or longer to complete. As tourists, we appreciate the amazing qualities of detail and workmanship that went into these massive commitments. Unfortunately, long-term commitments have become a thing of the past. Most jobs, contracts, or investments focus on short-term gain. To be committed is almost to appear stupid or naïve. I hear comments like, "I don't want to be locked in," or, "Who knows how I'll feel in two years." This thinking has penetrated both business decisions and relationships. Husbands and wives divorce and remarry quickly, family members hold to obligatory displays of loyalty or tradition as if tortured. In fact, the word *commitment* is seen as negative and antiquated to most "enlightened" people.

There was an all-time-high divorce rate in the early 1980s of up to 60 percent, but in the last two decades divorce has declined slightly. One report done by the National Marriage project suggests that the rate of divorce in the 1990s was between 40 and 45 percent. Nevertheless, I find it puzzling how a serious contract such as marriage can be broken so often by so many.

I believe commitment disappears first, then the fighting begins. I've witnessed some fights in my office that would raise the hair on your neck. They've included door-slamming, wall-kicking, pillow-throwing, mind games, and facial expressions all designed to trash each other. Couples who have settled the "commitment" issue do not destroy each other this way. It reminds me of a comment from a Vietnam veteran client who said, "You don't tick off the guy fighting in the trenches with you."

Marriage relationships parallel military partnerships. Now, I am not talking about a wife asking her husband to drop and give her "20," on the contrary, when at war, you must rely on your partner to watch your back. In marriage, as in war, you must trust your partner to be there for you. When faith in that contract is gone, all confidence disappears. This is why I witness couples at their worst. With commitment gone, all that's left is pure emotional pain. When commitment is not available to secure the relationship in a crisis, repair is almost impossible. Most of my early sessions with couples are spent assessing commitment. The best method of understanding desire, dedication, and determination for commitment is to pose three powerful questions.

**Desire**

One of the most powerful questions you can ask yourself or someone else is "*What do you want*?" This simple arrangement of words can lead to magical places in our wish files. When the answer to this question identifies a special person, then desire serves as potent motivation for success. Webster's dictionary defines desire as "a conscious impulse toward something that promises enjoyment or satisfaction in its attainment."

The energy created by desire has been known to move people to incredible accomplishments. I think of Kennedy's challenge to put a man on the moon before the end of the 1960s. A young man named Michael desired to be a great basketball player despite missing the cut his sophomore year of high school. Another man's desire to harness lightning by flying a kite changed how we experience our world during the dark half of the day. Two brothers saw a bird flying and their hearts soared at the possibilities. Desire stirs passion. Desire makes us willing to pay any price.

I think about the desire that stirred my passion to pursue my own marital union. I remember thinking, "If she would only marry me, my meager existence would be upgraded to dream status." The desire to marry Jana Sherrow was as strong a desire as I've ever known. I worked for every date. I courted her as if she were the queen of England. She was the catch of a lifetime. What sort of silly chip did God place in my brain that would cause this kind of wonderful recklessness?

The desire to mate is designed for us to live out our passions and experience the best He created for us. When you think of desire, what images come to your mind? Do you think of chocolate? Do you think of a new car? How about a different career? Whatever comes to mind, can you imagine ever attaining that goal without wanting it? Would you live in the home or drive the car you have now if you didn't experience desire first? Likewise, knowing what pulls you toward your partner can be sifted out by viewing the partnership through your lens of desire.

The marriage relationship can be fun and painful as well as exciting and draining. In unhealthy marriages, the desire to be right conquers the desire to be effective. In healthy marriages, the desire to cooperate prevails over the desire of one member to have control. Either way, desire controls the outcome.

Desire typically drives the train. That's why desire is the first of three powerful words that lead to commitment. When clients tell me they want a better marriage, I first ask them to define what that means. Common responses might be "more sex," "better communication," or "more fun together." Like ordering dinner from a restaurant, just wanting food doesn't produce the desired outcome. You must first select exactly what will appease your appetite, order it, then experience it satisfy the desire. Naming your desire is the first priority.

A relationship will only function properly when there is compatibility of desires. For instance, I worked with a couple who was having a sexual problem. The husband's desire for sex every day was so strong that it became his only priority. His wife complied, but she lost herself in the process.

When they tacitly agreed to daily sex they both denied her desire *not* to have sex all the time. When her desire was ignored, she became detached. Their relationship was shaped around this one desired goal, excluding any other desires that might be fulfilling to both of them. Eight years later she was so dissatisfied, she threatened to leave him and end the marriage. His desire to be close to his wife and enjoy the benefits that sex provided almost cost him the whole relationship. We worked hard to rearrange their priorities to include a better balance of honoring each others needs without compromising their personal integrity.

The couple asked me what they should have mutually agreed to in order to preserve their relationship. I suggested that in a relationship you want to agree to cooperation, trust, effective communication, and loyalty. These are the links that create fabulous sex and many other fantastic moments. The desire for sex is an incredible opportunity for couples to explore when that desire is cradled by supporting values. This couple was able to recognize that when sex is coupled with friendship, listening, and many other forms of intimacy, they became closer and more united.

A great illustration of the importance of keeping priorities was explained to me at a seminar. The story illustrates the difference between things that are important and things that are urgent. (Like deciding between spending time returning phone calls or reading a book your spouse recommended.) He showed his team an empty jar. Beside the jar were different sized stones. To fit all the stones in the jar, the big ones had to go first. Then, the smaller stones filled in the spaces. He then asked the team if the jar appeared full. When they affirmed it was full, he reached under the table and brought out a jar of sand. He then proceeded to pour sand into the jar, filling in more space between the stones. He asked again if the jar was full. Nobody answered. He then grabbed a pitcher of water and began filling the jar of sand and stones. His point was that once you get the important things taken care of, you'll get more out of your life than you ever imagined.

To become aware of important desires, you will have to know yourself. What do you want from your marriage? If having a big house is high priority, ask yourself why? What does it do for you? Perhaps you are looking for acceptance. Or you need affirmation. Regardless of the findings, typically what you want most camouflages a deeper desire. Discovering that deeper desire will give your marriage a better chance of remaining committed to each other. When the bigger desires are being fulfilled, there will be more time to explore the smaller wants and finer details of the relationship.

We all want to be loved, accepted, and needed. I daily embrace the wisdom of this. If accumulating wealth is your greatest desire, ask why? What will that do for you? Having money gets you power, which may help you to become famous. You can acquire friends, which would get you accepted or needed. Most desires are motivated by deeper longings. Unfortunately, many men and women never gain this insight. They chase after their hearts' desires making shallow attempts at filling a deep well. This activity is also quite common among married couples. While mindless energy is spent searching for things that don't satisfy, the relationship is robbed of necessary nurturing.

One young couple had been married four years when they came to me for counseling because they were not communicating with each other. When I helped them unravel their story, I discovered that she believed the "big stone" in their marriage jar was her career. As it turned out, he had agreed to support her, and moved with her outside the country to support her career as a journalist. Later, she made a career change to become a teacher that required them to move back to the States. He again agreed to support her, but with a request of his own. He wanted to start a family in two years. She agreed and began student teaching.

Things didn't go as planned (they often don't), and when it came time to start a family, she wasn't ready. He pushed and she pushed back. This pushing became very intense and eventually destroyed the marriage. They came to my office on the pretense of saving their marriage, but what they really wanted was permission to end it. After three sessions, they announced their decision to divorce and thanked me for my assistance.

As I look back on that relationship, I can now see they desired to be married, but they put the smaller rocks of career in the jar before the big "marriage rocks" of commitment were secured. The relationship wasn't strong enough to weather the stress of moving to a foreign country, changing careers, and absorbing major disappointments. I believe they were both sincere in desiring a great marriage. Nevertheless, they made commitment to a great marriage secondary to satisfying career goals.

Sometimes couples discover this in time to rearrange their priorities. One such couple found that their priorities changed when they began having children. She focused on caring for two toddlers, and he found refuge in working more. When they came to me they were ready to give up. We discussed what their early commitments were to each other and listed their dreams and aspirations. After five or six sessions discussing their desires and reconnecting them to the passion of their relationship, they regained hope. Their bigger priority was being overlooked by the allurement of parenting responsibilities.

Desire can breathe passion into the life of a long-term relationship. Detecting those desires is sometimes difficult in the daily distractions of tedious duties, so that we tend to replace wishes and desires with "I have to" and "I can't." I read a relevant article entitled "Simplify Your Life" in *Kiplinger's Personal Finance* magazine, an unlikely source for personal growth and inspiration. The article suggests, "Most people are in a rut, doing what they are expected to rather than what they want to do."[1] The article profiled people learning to live with less, to gain balance, time with families, and passion. Take inventory of your marriage and discover if your, "I have to's" and "I want to's" are properly aligned.

The goal of desire is to make the connection between what you want and what you are willing to do to get it and keep it. The action of desire usually weeds out the wannabes. Desire can last a lifetime if properly maintained. To make it as authentic and sincere as it was at the beginning, we need to regularly revisit the source of our desire through reflection and focus.

To maintain focus on a goal, spontaneous reminders can be helpful. Olympic athletes, for example, train for years to test their skills. How do they maintain high levels of desire? I imagine a coach and teammates ignite desire by keeping the vision of gold medals alive. As it says in Proverbs, "Where there is no vision the people will perish."

Large companies hold meetings, buy pens and mugs, hold golf outings, print mottoes on T-shirts to keep desire alive. Why would it be different in a marriage relationship? Couples must be proactive about keeping desire a high priority. First you set the goal and then you rally emotional fuel to support it. Wouldn't it be great if couples printed T-shirts with a logo of their love desire? Or every three months couples held a golf outing or getaway weekend in honor of their marriage vows? Can you imagine pens lying around the house imprinted with the saying, "Listen first, then listen some more"? Such outward symbols of commitment are bound to have positive results.

**Dedication**

The next powerful question is: "What will it do for you?" Webster's dictionary defines dedication as "devotion to a cause or purpose." I can see now why my high school basketball coach wanted us dedicated. He knew we would be tempted by distractions ranging from high school parties, drugs and alcohol, girls, to other vices. To play on his team we had to be fully devoted.

Scripture has many examples of being dedicated to an important cause. I am reminded of Paul's words in Hebrews 12:1–4:

> Do you see what this means—all these pioneers who blazed the way, all these veterans cheering us on? It means we'd better get on with it. Strip down, start running—and never quit! No extra spiritual fat, no parasitic sins. Keep your eyes on Jesus, who both began and finished this race we're in. Study how he did it. Because he never lost sight of where he was headed—that exhilarating finish in and with God—he could put up with anything along the way: cross, shame, whatever. And now he's there, in the place of honor, right alongside God. *(The Message Bible)*

The dedication to a race parallels that of marriage. In part, you must want to run the race, next you must devote yourselves to it, and last be determined to finish. This illustration of what it takes to be a Christ follower also gives partners in marriage a model to keep them steady.

Marital devotion requires us to decide upon our combined purpose as a couple and remain devoted to it. The purpose question is, "What will it do for you?" A devoted heart must be clear about its devotion. Happiness is not a purpose. If anything, happiness is just a passing product of good luck. Couples often think their purpose is to make each other or themselves happy. The purpose or "mission statement" of marriage provides the motivation if it is clear and meaningful. Have you ever thought about what your marital purpose is? What does being married add to your life? As a couple, take a moment after reading this section and write out your answers.

I've asked couples at workshops and retreats what the purpose of their marriage is. The answers are typically very vague and hard to put into words. Common answers include: to make each other happy, to raise children, to share a life. These are fine goals, but not concrete. Such elusive concepts can have a different meaning for each person, leading to general dissatisfaction and miscommunication. If you tell your brain you want to make your wife happy, what will the response be? Perhaps your brain will direct you to your wife's favorite recreation, or accomplishing a chore to please her. Your brain can't act on an undefined concept. Adler once said, "We cannot think, feel, will, or act without the perception of some goal."[2] Defining a marriage's purpose is the keystone of devotion.

If a pastor asked two engaged couples why they're marrying, they would probably give two different answers. Let's say the first couple says, "To live happily ever after." The second couple responds, "We would like to honor each other daily, serve Christ together, work hard, have a couple of children, and enjoy frequent vacations together." Which couple has the better chance of meeting their goal? The second couple broke down their desire for happiness into doable, concrete actions. Married couples who live "on purpose" will find fulfillment. Those who don't will be frustrated and discontented.

The wedding ceremony itself is a form of dedication. Vows are the purpose statement of marriage. Can you remember them? "I Bob/Janet take this man/woman to be my lawfully wedded husband/wife, to have and to hold from this day forward, for better for worse, for richer, for poorer, in sickness and in health, forsaking all others, to cling only to him/her, for as long as we both shall live, or our Lord doth come." This ceremony is a wonderful dedication. Concrete words describe devotion to a long-lasting, potentially complicated, emotionally and physically connected adventure.

Scott Stanley, in his book *The Heart of Commitment*, describes commitment as having two different expressions. Over years of research he found that commitment can be expressed as *dedication* or *constraint*. Listen for the difference in the following example.

Frank and Mary stay in their marriage for different reasons. Frank is an attorney and he believes a contract is binding and he should keep his promise. Mary takes offense to Frank's position. She feels deeply committed to him emotionally, and would not leave him because of her intense emotional connection.

Each is equally committed to the other. They find themselves discussing their peculiar perspectives. She interprets his standpoint as a cold, calculated reason to stay together. He believes her to be emotionally irrational. This is not unusual.

Dedication is the devotion to a cause or purpose. Constraint, according to Webster, is "a state of being checked, restricted, or compelled to avoid or perform some action." Dedication implies a movement toward something and constraint implies movement away from something. Stanley suggests, "If dedication is a force drawing you forward, constraint is a force pushing you from behind."[3] When I read this, I see a man and a woman. She is leaning forward tugging her husband's hand with a smile on her face. He is leaning back, but willingly following because something is kicking him from behind. Ted Millon, a psychologist and personality theorist believes we are all motivated to either avoid pain or increase pleasure. He developed a polarity theory of personality that is based on the concept that we all aim for one of these two goals.[4] However, when we are too focused on one extreme, we find ourselves out of balance. Just like the pain/pleasure principle, neither dedication nor constraints are all good or all bad.

The reality of marriage is that over time you will have constraints, some more potent than others. The constraint of divorce is more powerful when large sums of money are involved. This is also true when there are children involved. Most couples talk more cautiously about the ramifications of divorce when these two variables are present.

The constraint commitment may be stronger for women to cook meals and clean house when their mother-in-law was a traditional housewife. Dedication on the other hand is both the fuel and the essence of commitment. You can imagine that when both dedication and commitment are present, the marriage bond is strong, like the push and pull motion of the pedals on a bike. Opposite motions synchronize to propel the bike forward.

Dedication is something you can build on; constraints are just consequences of married life. Remember your idea of a constraint may or may not be reality.

Frank and Mary did not think much about their constraint commitment until their children went away to college and they focused on the condition of their marriage. After twenty-seven years of marriage, a fully vested 401K, and financial responsibilities, Frank found the complications of the marriage manageable. Mary, however, realized that the heartfelt dedication commitment had eroded. She is working desperately to regain passion while he is attempting to avoid a breakup. This push and pull was keeping them together but causing them both to feel misunderstood and miserable. Their need to fix the problem in different ways agitated each other like salt and vinegar. Frank and Mary need to agree that twenty-seven years of marriage is worth discovering a new focus for their marriage. The constraints can then serve the new mutual goal rather than negate it. A marriage dedicated to fulfilling its goals and dreams can keep the coals of commitment hot.

**Determination**

Once desire discovers its want, and dedication has its purpose, raw determination is what makes it happen. The third powerful question is, "How are you going to do it?" The biblical reference to a race, noted earlier in this section, provided a model for starting and finishing your goal.

One of the most grueling human races, is a marathon—26.2 miles of constant movement. Marathon runners face aching muscles, hours of training, and goofy body experiences such as lost toenails, bleeding nipples, and various skin rashes. When they are heavily focused on their goal, they can enter a place they call "the zone." This zone is a mental arena for the thoughts and emotions of a person attempting to run a full marathon.

I can't imagine a more vivid example of determination. I have a friend who has run in several marathons. She tells me that the last few miles of a marathon are accomplished through sheer determination and adrenalin. When the runner finds herself just a few miles away from the end, she is focused on only one thing no matter the obstacles: finishing.

What would happen if we applied this kind of commitment to the institution of marriage? People commit to running a marathon for no reason other than to finish. Imagine what could happen if couples tapped their own source of determination to finish and finish well in marriage challenges. Unlike running, marriage has so much more to offer. The determination to finish a marriage is loaded with possibilities.

Knowing what you want from marriage, then identifying the purpose, leads you to explore how you will achieve your goals. The actions that keep marriage alive are both energizing and draining.

I am not exactly sure what motivates people to finish marathons, unravel a tangled slinky, or stay married for a lifetime. The clear common denominator is perseverance. When I have occasion to ask couples who have been married for more than fifty years how they did it, they usually say something about just hanging in there. Research of couples who have been married over twenty-five years suggest they work hard at teamwork.

Webster defines determination as "the act of deciding definitely and firmly" or "the power or habit of deciding definitely and firmly." It would be easy to focus on the actions of a determined person, but the real power is in their resolution.

Perhaps the most salient trait needed to sustain marriage is the decision to do so. I know that most divorced individuals believed that they would be married forever. In fact they probably felt they had made "the decision" of a lifetime. In many divorces, there is one who wants to stay and fight for the marriage. Unfortunately, determination must come from both husband and wife.

Being committed to a lifelong marriage requires saying no to any opportunities that subordinate the marriage. I believe one temptation comes in the form of new opportunities. I have had men explain to me why they cheated on their wife with this argument, "I didn't think anyone like her would ever be attracted to me." A new opportunity creates anxiety about thinking we missed something to which we are entitled. The feeling of missing something is of course only relevant if you keep that option open.

For many people, intimacy with their mate is foreign. They are tempted by the promise of intimacy in a different relationship. If partners are determined in their decision to be committed, then the focus will remain on creating intimacy in their marriage rather than finding it elsewhere.

I would like to end this chapter with a quote from a man I believe understands the concept of commitment, at least in terms of sports.

"I always believed that if you put in the work, the results will come. I don't do things halfheartedly. Because I know if I do, then I can expect halfhearted results. That's why I approached practices the same way I approached games. You can't turn it on and off like a faucet. I couldn't dog it during practice and then, when I needed that extra push late in the game, expect it to be there. But that's how a lot of people approach things. They sound like they're committed to being the best they can be. They say all the right things, and make all the proper appearances. But when it comes right down to it, they're looking for reasons instead of answers."[5] —Michael Jordan, *I Can't Accept Not Trying*.

Michael Jordan brought his commitment to basketball and made a huge impact. I challenge you to live out your commitment to your marriage and experience the impact desire, dedication, and determination can have on your relationship.

"Desire is the key to motivation, but it's determination and commitment to an unrelenting pursuit of your goal—a commitment to excellence—that will enable you to attain the success you seek." *—Mario Andretti*

COMMITMENT
CAPABILITIES
Chapter Summary
RED
Only commit to what's good for you.
YELLOW
Be fully committed as long as your partner is.
GREEN
Give everything you can to the relationship.

*Chapter Six*

# Comfortably Close

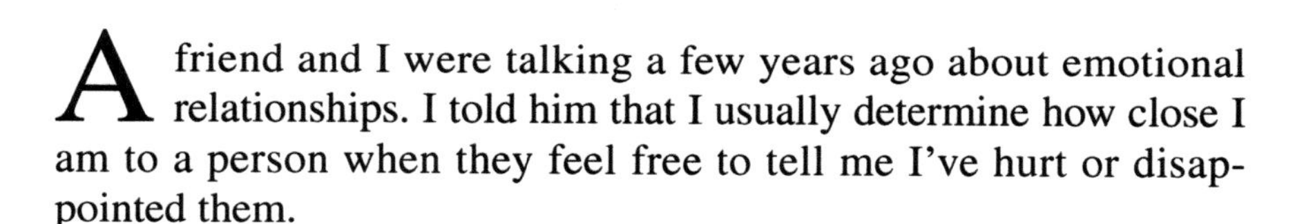

A friend and I were talking a few years ago about emotional relationships. I told him that I usually determine how close I am to a person when they feel free to tell me I've hurt or disappointed them.

My friend replied, "Yep, and for me that's when we are no longer friends."

The closeness task involves intimate connections, warm feelings, and empathic communication. For many reasons, couples have struggled with this task by the time they reach my office. One motivation for seeking counseling is that one or both partners "feel" bad about the relationship. I hear comments like, "I love my wife, but I am not *in love* with my wife," or "I love him, but like a brother." When I ask how long they've felt this way, the response is usually, "For a long time…uh…maybe since we got married."

Sadly some couples lose closeness as soon as they begin performing their marriage roles. I remember one couple telling me that it was as if a light switched off as soon as they returned from their honeymoon. Rather than thinking it strange, they both dove into their roles, convinced that marriage was supposed to be this way. They came to see me because the wife found herself drawn to a man at work. As she explored her marriage relationship, she realized she was not experiencing an emotional connection. When she brought this up to her husband, he agreed and they both reached out for help.

Isolation is a major problem in troubled marriages, not to mention a few "good" marriages. When partners don't feel close, they often pursue other outlets for their intimacy needs. These outlets may include jobs, hobbies, food, or other relationships. Regardless of the diversion, energy can escape the primary emotional outlet—the partner. David Olsen organized and conducted the *National Survey of Marital Strengths* and reported them at a marriage conference in 2001.[1] He surveyed more than twenty thousand couples in happy marriages from all fifty states. The research identified the top ten characteristics of happily married couples. "Closeness" was in the top five marital strengths.

These results lead me to believe that couples who enjoy their marriages are finding ways to complete the task of feeling close. This is not a surprise because feeling close leads to deeper levels of intimacy. I have discovered three paths that lead to creating closeness—revealing, receiving, and risking. Read about the three paths and discover what you are doing well or can improve in order for your marriage to deepen intimacy.

**Revealing: Marriage Masks**

There's something appealing and mysterious about masks. When we wear masks, we revel in the chance to be someone we are not. There have been so many situations when I have dreamed of being someone else. The allure is subtle, but present. Some women hide their flaws with excessive makeup; some men hide behind expensive suits and nice cars. When we determine to hide ourselves, we believe we protect ourselves from ridicule or embarrassment. Larry Crabb, author and psychologist, says, "No matter how together we may appear, even to ourselves, buried deep within our heart is a vague sense that something is wrong, dreadfully wrong."[2]

We spend most of our youth working to appear normal so that our friends and family respond to us casually. As long as we maintain a cool, attractive image, no one will bother to probe into our inner life.

Any relationship is limited to how authentic the people are who build it. If the contributions to the Us are false, then partners have succeeded in creating an Us mask as well. Hence, the Us mask is just an image of a false identity.

Wearing multiple masks can be difficult. I've worked with couples who strive to hide their therapy from everyone, even their own families. They are usually unable to succeed in the cover-up because their nagging struggles expose themselves at the most awkward times. Our masks are primarily important to us because we typically overestimate the reaction of our peers to our concealed flaws. Yet, most folks are too preoccupied with hiding their own imperfections to notice those of others. Regardless of this knowledge, we still fear the risk of exposure.

While minding my own business in church one day, I found myself in conversation with a struggling couple. This couple made great sacrifices in relocating for the husband's job, only to lose it six months later. They were walking around church that day hurting deeply but attempting to mask it. It only took asking one probing question to bring the wife to tears. I thought to myself that church, of all places, should be a place where we can drop our masks at the door. This besieged couple needed to be supported by their church community. However, they chose to mask their pain and attempt to appear as though they were fine. Stoicism was not a virtue, in this case. I'm convinced that the masks won't come off until compassion and empathy are valued over image and success.

When my son, Seth, began fifth grade, he was unconcerned with trying to be "somebody." He was perfectly content with himself. Sometimes he frustrated my wife and me because he wouldn't succumb to *our* need to shape him. Can you imagine a son of a psychologist not following the program? We determined to let him be himself, while providing the appropriate social training. With adolescence right around the corner, we expect him to be ridiculed or lured into being just like everyone else. Everything he'll experience in the next few years will directly challenge his precious self-expression. He will fight to swim upstream and maintain his own voice throughout his teen years. It will be a challenge for him to make it to college without a shaky sense of self. His journey is filled with emotional ups and downs right now.

Although some adolescents want to be different, most of them will not risk being authentic. I believe most masks worn by adults are fabricated between the ages of twelve and eighteen. Unveiling these masks can be nearly impossible because they are so strongly tied to acceptance achieved during high school. It's common for college to perpetuate these masks. Many people acquire their jobs and marriages by selling their masks, not their true selves.

How can we expect our children to be healthy, integrated human beings when they build their identities on false impressions and fictional personalities? For my son's sake, and for hundreds of young couples, there needs to be safe harbors where people can remove their masks and make real connections.

### *Personality Masks*

Personality assessments are wonderful tools for understanding and learning about people. However, they can also be used as clever excuses for inappropriate behavior. As a psychologist, I'm trained to administer diagnostic assessments. They provide professionals a way to classify problems. When professionals study psychological functioning, a common language and labeling system helps identify behavior patterns.

During graduate school this was my favorite topic. For some reason, it builds confidence in a novice therapist's mind to be able to label a pattern of behavior concisely. We're trained to find problems and claim them as if scoring a basketball goal. Yet, when we tell our client the great news that we have discovered their "problem," they don't cheer like they would at a basketball game. For training therapists, as well as the average person, this preoccupation with labels is hard to resist. When I offer workshops, people are always most interested in personality themes. This fascination captures the essence of what I mean by personality masks. Once we discover a label that fits, we can blame our behavior on the label, rather than take responsibility for our own choices.

The new label can become something to hide behind, another mask. A partner will say to a spouse, "You know I am an introvert and don't like to share my feelings," or, "You knew when you married me I was outgoing and liked to talk to other women." One time a woman said to her husband, "Dr. McKinley told you I was a [busy] Beaver personality and you just have to deal with me, 'cause that's the way I am." It is these types of comments that interfere with relationship progress.

Understanding your personality style gives you insight, self-awareness, and a reference for your behavior. Your personality can express your values and beliefs or provide a diversion to protect you. If you think people should like you because you are basically nice and have a "pleasant personality," then you may be wearing a personality mask to cover up your real self who is sometimes *not* pleasant.

Some couples hide behind the mask of personality to avoid doing relationship work. They will enjoy the relationship when they find their common ground in beliefs and values rather than focusing on their varied means of expression. When we mislead loved ones to gain acceptance via masks, it ultimately leads to rejection. Personality styles are a natural part of the relationship challenge. Couples will benefit by not using their personality to hide uncomfortable feelings. If you speak honestly and candidly to each other, your personality style will be less likely to derail communication.

***Role Masks***

Like personality masks, role masks are convenient escapes for people to hide behind. Men in America argue convincingly that they have to be at work fifty-plus hours per week or they will lose their jobs. The role of "provider" takes priority over household roles. When have you heard of a family relocating because the home caretaker needed a promotion? I can hear it now, "If we moved to Cleveland, the mothers in that neighborhood would allow us to keep the home profitable." No. We give priority to the provider.

Do the majority of parents take their parenting role seriously? What value do they place on its importance? I once coached a mid-level executive who clearly informed his boss that his family took priority. He chose not to sacrifice his family for his job. How many homes would benefit from men and women setting that boundary? The traditional role-based marriage has been around for years. The advantage of this marriage type is that each person knows what they are expected to do. It reduces arguments about daily roles, such as who does the dishes, and who takes out the garbage. Of course, everyone doesn't fit into the traditional roles. A recently remarried couple I worked with found themselves in the following argument:

| | |
|---|---|
| *Husband:* | "She wanted to have a baby and now she has what she wants." |
| *Wife:* | "I can't do all the laundry, dishes, housework, and baby care without his help." |
| *Husband:* | "I do the yard work and fix things around the house, that's it." |
| *Wife:* | (Crying) "I just don't understand why he doesn't want to support me and the baby." |
| *Husband:* | "She got exactly what she wanted." |
| *Wife:* | (Crying, no response) |

What's unfortunate about this dialogue is that both partners are rigidly role-defined, yet with the addition of a baby, she's got more work to do. Before having the baby, her role was to take care of the housework. Now that the baby is here, she is using her new role to leverage his help. When the roles you play become so intertwined with who you are, you are unlikely to build intimacy. You want to maintain clarity about who you are while serving your required role. A better approach for this request might be for the woman to ask her husband what part in baby care would he like to be involved in.

Roles are useful and productive in defining boundaries that keep the relationship safe. The identified roles can produce clarity and a sense of purpose to each partner. However, when the relationship becomes role-defined, it leaves you vulnerable to infections of selfishness and pride that weaken the marriage. This happens when your role is used as a mask; then the relationship is endangered by neglect. It makes me think of Andy's deputy, Barney, on *The Andy Griffith Show*. He was scared of his own shadow, but his role as a police officer forced him to act as if he were brave. The humor of his character was in the obvious gap between his role and who he really was. Don't allow your role to inadvertently create a gap in your marriage.

***Family of Origin Masks***

*A married couple was in a terrible accident where the man's face was severely burned. The doctor told the husband that they couldn't graft any skin from his body because he was too skinny.*

*So the wife offered to donate some of her own skin. However, the only skin on her body that the doctor felt was suitable would have to come from her buttocks. The husband and wife agreed that they would tell no one about where the skin came from, and requested the doctor also honor their secret. After all, this was a very delicate matter.*

*After the surgery was completed, everyone was amazed at the man's new look. He looked better than he had ever had before! All his friends and relatives just went on and on about his youthful face!*

*One day, he was alone with his wife, and he was overcome with emotion at her sacrifice. He said, "Honey, I just want to thank you for everything you did for me. There is no way I could ever repay you." She replied, "That's fine honey, you can't believe the satisfaction I get every time I see your mother kiss your cheek."*

Using humor to cope with family patterns can add temporary relief. However, far too often someone gets hurt. Joking about family members and their ways of doing things is part of every marriage. The reality is we all come from very different situations that hold special meaning to us. What many people do not realize is how those differences impact their marriage. Lack of self-awareness is the leading cause for this marital mask.

Characteristics developed by childhood experiences can be considered a primary marriage block for some relationships. Family of origin is a psychology term used to express patterns of thinking and behavior learned in childhood. I remember the first time I realized not all families use fans as sleep aids at night. A nightly ritual for the McKinley family was to get out a twenty-six–inch box fan and turn it on high. As you can imagine, this was surprising to my new bride. She went from quiet nights to a bed partner with a strange habit. It would have been easy for me to just tell her the fan stays, regardless. I could have said, "This is the way I've always done it." Instead, we discussed the reason for using a sleeping aid and compared them against the adjustments she would have to make if we kept the fan. The fan stayed, and now we have two children hooked! Conversely, when either partner uses childhood rituals as an excuse or mask, the relationship is destined to be superficial. Jana and I, like many couples, have to wrangle with those "sacred cows" and put them into perspective.

Sometimes, spouses don't know their family-of-origin issues are surfacing. Their partner will notice the pattern in a look or an attitude. They may also show up as an addiction or other self-destructive behavior. Since it is common to identify problems in others more readily than in ourselves, we'll tend to notice things about our partner's family early on in the relationship. Some couples tell me they don't want to say anything because they think it won't change anything. Other couples have told me they started fighting about family-of-origin issues before they were ever married.

Family-of-origin baggage always impacts relationships. No one lives with the same people for eighteen years without there being significant impact on habits, characteristics, and behaviors. Many traits that partners love in their spouses are blended with odd family quirks.

When you excuse behaviors with, "I'm like this because of my mother, so you can't hold it against me," you're deceiving yourself with a family-of-origin mask. You are a product of a family environment and gene pool. Even so, you are free and capable of autonomous functioning, which includes changing bad habits learned at home if they don't serve your adult relationships. Family-of-origin issues are among the top reasons why marriages fail. You can begin changing them by learning how to redirect unwanted messages from childhood. You start this by identifying useful and outdated beliefs. Make a list of the beliefs or habits that cause the most conflict with your spouse. Then ask yourself which ones are you willing to fight for and why. It can be difficult to change long-term habits, but it's worth the effort to try. It can be freeing and open the door to intimacy.

**Receiving**

There is an outdoor game that teaches this lesson well. It is called the egg-toss game. Two people play catch with an egg. They start out a few feet apart and then back up one step after each toss. The object of the game is to not let the egg break in your hands. The further apart you get, the more likely the egg will break. Each player learns quickly they have to catch the egg softly by cradling the egg in motion.

This is what receiving each other in marriage needs to imitate. When something like a rotten egg is being thrown your way, it is your job to receive it in the best possible manner. Let's face it. Sometimes what you get is going to make a mess no matter what you do. Other times, you can soften the landing by cradling your partner's offensive action. Relationship flexibility is crucial for any hope in being a good "egg-toss player."

Wanting to join a fitness center, I went in for a physical fitness test. The evaluation was flying, until I was told to sit down and place my feet into this strange contraption that tested flexibility. The instructor told me to hold my hands and arms out straight, keep my knees locked, and push a little bar as far as I could. I leaned forward and started pushing the bar smoothly until all at once a loud cry unexpectedly came from my mouth. The instructor said, "Go ahead, you can start now." He was laughing, but I reached my breaking point and nothing was going to convince me to push any further. The instructor encouraged me with, "You can go farther than that!" I'm very competitive, so I tried again. He smiled sympathetically and politely wrote something down. I was crushed.

Later I asked him why flexibility was so important. He replied that muscle and tendon flexibility allows you to work the muscle groups harder without injury. With greater flexibility, the workout won't harm your joints. This reminds me of how remaining flexible in marriage is good for similar reasons. Rigidity often leads to relational injury.

According to the study done by Olsen, couple flexibility is one of the top five strengths in happy marriages. The trends found in this study serve as a good template for remaining relationally flexible and able to receive your partner softly. There are five characteristics for flexibility. They are *adjusting to change*, *flexibility in lifestyle*, *making most decisions jointly, creatively handling issues,* and *compromising on differences.* As you think about these five strengths, you quickly realize why they are important in receiving each other.

***Adjusting to Change***

One thing is always true about change: no one likes it. People create comfort zones with their attitudes and behaviors and are very protective of them.

Have you ever heard this from a hard-working employee? A worker is asked to launch a project. He spends months designing and implementing it. Then, just as it's fully implemented, a new director comes in with new ideas and scraps the whole project. The worker is later criticized for his unsupportive behavior during the transition.

Marriages host similar rapid cycling of continuous change and pressure. Most couples today are faced with hundreds of tasks, demands, and activities every month with challenging time constraints. Flexibility is paramount to managing change.

***Flexibility in Lifestyle***

Couples argue every day when one person won't give up their way of doing things. This ranges from bedtime rituals to decorating to how to pack a picnic lunch.

Lifestyle flexibility can radically improve couple closeness. If a woman is willing to forgo or delay her evening TV show to go on a "drive to nowhere" with her husband, amazing things can happen. Lifestyle complaints are the most common ones in marriage. My father-in-law developed a motto while raising children to keep him from blowing a gasket. "If it's not immoral, illegal, fattening, or dangerous, let it go." This was his way of prioritizing his parenting values. Rather than battling everything, he decided to let his children find their own way unless it affected their souls, their physical health, or their freedom.

Marriages would benefit by following this motto. Decide what your marital values are and hold each other accountable to them. Anything that falls outside of your list, let it go.

### *Making Joint Decisions*

Making successful joint decisions is work. Just think of naming children. How many children have been named through compromise? Most couples take a Cooperative I stance when faced with joint decisions. For example, couples may let the wife make decisions about the children and the husband make decisions about money. This may work for some things, but when bigger issues come up, the couple may not have the practice of working in concert.

What will you do, for example, when your teenage daughter discloses that she is pregnant? Because this is so personal and women rally during this time, do you, as the dad, just stay out of the way? If you do, you may appear disinterested. These difficult problems require couples to work together and develop partnering skills to make good decisions.

There are many decisions in a relationship that can be made without each other, but the practice and skill of making joint decisions is too important to avoid. Buying houses, changing jobs, making major purchases, having children, and choosing a church are all examples of unavoidable joint decisions.

Collaborating may be difficult, but it is certainly attainable. Susan Heitler, in her book *The Power of Two,* says, "Without collaborative problem solving, decisions that affect both of you can easily trigger negative reactions from minor irritation to large upheaval."[3] There are ways to work together if you acknowledge one another's perspectives, communicate effectively, and negotiate your battle lines wisely.

### *Creatively Handling Issues*

This is discussed more thoroughly in the "Cooperation Challenge" chapter. A helpful hint is to see your partner as trustworthy and competent, even if he or she is opposing you. Begin discussions with respect and openness. If your partner is manipulative or selfish, then negotiation will be a problem anyway. If working things out appears impossible, then seek professional help to negotiate.

Most issues can be navigated with gentleness, understanding, and clear communication. I also want to point out the word "creative." Creatively handling issues implies you are considering new methods when old ones no longer work. Dakota tribal wisdom says it well: "When you discover you are riding a dead horse, the best strategy is to dismount."

Look at the problem from a different perspective. I have suggested some outrageous things to couples in the past. If perspective is your problem, try climbing onto the roof of your house together and discuss the issue there. Role-play each other's position for a while. Strip down to your underwear and try to argue about it while cleaning toilets. Whatever you do, avoid the same fruitless conversation patterns.

***Compromising the Differences***

Compromise is a useful skill for CI marriages, but Us marriages can usually handle differences without it. While there are times when it's appropriate to let your partner lead, a compromise is often a lose-lose scenario. I would rather have couples understand each other and yield to their differences. Find a win-win solution.

With compromise, you are both saying, "I'll give up something." Acknowledgment and acceptance is the key to differences. When the differences are causing problems in the relationship itself, then acknowledging them is a starting point. Once the problems are defined, a plan to correct them can be developed. Acceptance is difficult if both partners don't agree to solve problems actively. The old saying "If you're not part of the solution, you're part of the problem" states the point clearly.

Like the skills required to win at the egg-toss game, these five practices will allow you to carefully hear and attend to your partner. Couples who have mastery with these practices will inevitably experience closeness. As you make it a practice to reveal yourself to each other, learning to receive one another will perpetuate a close connection.

## Risking

*If You Want to Walk on Water, You Have to Get out of the Boat* is the title of a challenging book by John Ortberg. My risk-taking book would sound more like, *If You Want to Walk on Water, I Hope You Like Seaweed.* Some people I counsel are so fear-based that they are relationally crippled. It seems that by avoiding confrontation, we're rewarded for not sounding off the buzzer, as in the old *Operation* board game. This game tests your ability to pull body parts carefully out of holes without sounding a buzzer. The more careful you are, the more you win. My daughter Megan hates this game because she doesn't like to make mistakes, so she just quits playing. Relationships are like that sometimes—you don't want to make mistakes, so you carefully maneuver around a problem to prevent the "buzzer" from going off.

Relational risk is not only needed for intimacy, it is the purest form of intimacy. The more you risk opening up to your partner, the closer you'll feel. Although when you're open, you are also more vulnerable. That is why safety is so important. Consequently, safety is only developed as you risk vulnerability. It's a catch-22 where you have to step out in surrender at some point to have the best intimacy payoff. There are times when you hurt each other inadvertently. Nevertheless, you must continue taking risks to build trust and safety, which lead to closeness.

Fear-based activity is loaded with obstacles to intimacy. Behind every word or action is a possible "I told you so" or "I knew I shouldn't have tried that" lurking in the shadows. For years, psychologists have studied the effect of fear on self-concept. Compulsions based on the beliefs that "I have to" and "I can't" are deeply imprinted in the minds of fear-based people. Some examples of these beliefs include:

> *I have to finish my work today or I might get fired.*
> *I can't tell my wife about losing my job because she will get upset.*
> *I have to get the house clean to prove I'm a good wife.*
> *I can't tell her she upset me because it will hurt her feelings.*

Research suggests that just hearing these words is immobilizing. Everyone struggles with such self-talk. Couples who want a close relationship must overcome negative self-talk and risk their hearts for intimacy to develop. For most people, the idea of being completely honest with someone is ludicrous. I was doing a life-coaching seminar not too long ago and a woman stopped me at a break and said, "These questions we are asking of each other are too personal. I don't think we should be asking these questions of people we don't know. In fact, I wouldn't even tell my spouse some of these things." I discussed with her a bit further the need to clarify personal desires. She responded, "I don't want honesty from my husband if I have to tell him my secrets." I paused and sighed. I told her that as long as she keeps her pain locked up, she misses out on joy. She just walked away. This was a very unsettling conversation partly because I had no means to follow up with her. She didn't buy a word I said and likely wrote me off that very moment.

Many couples are stuck in this same place. They are holding dreams of intimacy hostage for the ransom of refusing exposure. Many people agree that the price of pain is too high to risk vulnerability. If you want to be close to your partner, there has to be honesty and openness, both of which are very risky.

I'll close this chapter by telling you about Sarah. We met while she was in the hospital. Sarah was in terrible emotional shape. Her psychiatrist treated her with anti-psychotic medication. She was suicidal, had bizarre thoughts, and was generally unresponsive to treatment. As one of her group therapists in the hospital, I began to draw her out a little each time she was in group with me.

Toward the end of her stay, I invited her to work with me privately once she was out of the hospital. I was pleasantly surprised when she called me about three weeks later. We began working together twice a week for many months. As I suspected she wasn't psychotic, rather she was suffering from Post-Traumatic Stress Disorder (PTSD). We uncovered a ten-year history of severe sexual abuse that occurred between the ages of six and sixteen. She had been molested, raped, and experienced ritualistic satanic sexual abuse. Her childhood was riddled with sexual violations. By contrast, she was living in the suburbs with five children, masquerading as the perfect mom. When the safe bubble fabricated to protect her burst, she literally came undone.

For months, she told me secrets she never intended to tell

anyone. One by one, we walked through her devastating experiences, hoping to stimulate healing. Though she had been married for eighteen years, she had no idea how lonely she was. Her marriage was built on smoke and mirrors. She was nothing like the person she pretended to be every day at home. She began rebuilding an authentic life for herself.

Week after week, I challenged her to risk breaking through deeply entrenched self-destructive patterns. Everything she did was risky. Teaming with me was her first major risk. She then had to learn to relate honestly to her husband and children. This was a horrifying experience for her sometimes. She found the therapeutic relationship her safe haven as we dismantled her fears one by one.

Sarah had spent years creating an alternate reality to accommodate her mistaken thinking. At one point she asked me if she was finally beginning to experience reality. I responded affirmatively that she was finally dealing with real issues and real people. With her head down she rolled her eyes up to me and said, "Yeah? Well, reality sucks." I paused for a moment and embraced her comment with empathy. Her greatest fear was to risk it all and then face rejection. Instead, she found out that working on her marriage was just plain hard work even without the risk of rejection. We realized she had finally made it over the hump. She was back with the rest of us just trying to connect to her spouse meaningfully. Her story gets better every year. She has inched her way into a relationship with her husband that is satisfying and growing. She still has a long way to go, but she would tell you to reveal your true self, receive your partner with an open mind, and risk being authentic. It's worth it.

"Intimacy is not a matter of extending your self-absorption to include someone else. Much more than that, it is a matter of tuning into someone else's reality, and risking being changed by that experience." —*Stephanie Dowrick,* Intimacy & Solitude

COMFORTABLY
CLOSE
Chapter Summary
RED
Do your best, but don't get hurt.
YELLOW
Share with your partner everything you can.
GREEN
Risk being hurt by courageous conversations.

*Section 3*

# FIT for Us

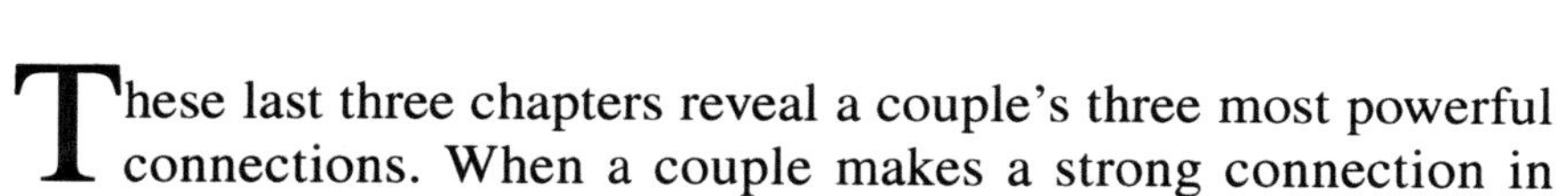

These last three chapters reveal a couple's three most powerful connections. When a couple makes a strong connection in these three areas of marriage, it builds a foundation that can support, guide, and sustain growth in all other marital areas.

*Focus* on Us.

*Invest* in Sex.

*Transcend* your Marriage.

The first chapter in this section, "Love R Us," directs couples in how to love the marital relationship itself. Loving a relationship requires a different focus than loving each other. You will learn how to love your relationship so that it can provide you with a lasting marriage that pays dividends beyond your expectations.

The second chapter, "Sex from the Us Position," encourages couples to invest in a healthy sexual connection. The sexual union is the pinnacle of marital satisfaction. Sexual relations distinguish marriage from all other significant relationships. If you want to enjoy the full benefits of marriage, challenge yourselves to cultivate an open, natural, and exciting sex life.

The last chapter, "Soul Mates," offers a penetrating look at the purpose of marriage. Do you live together to only serve each other's needs, or is there more for you? I challenge you to explore how God can help you transcend your marriage for His purposes. A spiritual connection can transform the average couple into life-long soul mates!

*Chapter Seven*

# Love R Us

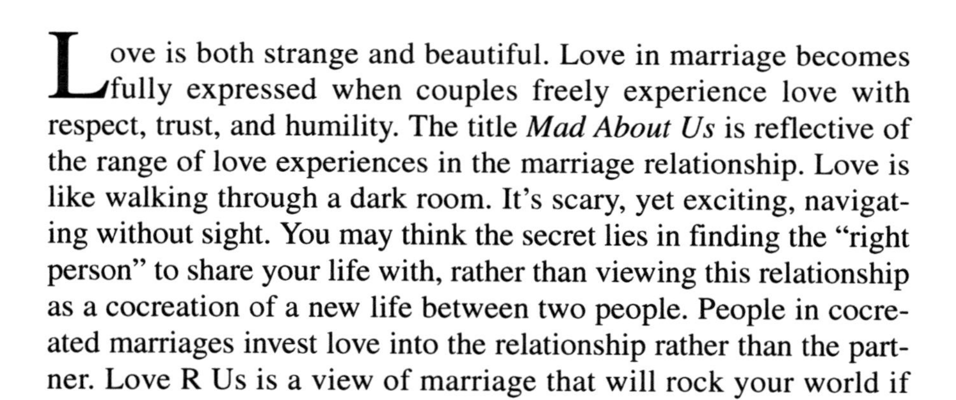

Love is both strange and beautiful. Love in marriage becomes fully expressed when couples freely experience love with respect, trust, and humility. The title *Mad About Us* is reflective of the range of love experiences in the marriage relationship. Love is like walking through a dark room. It's scary, yet exciting, navigating without sight. You may think the secret lies in finding the "right person" to share your life with, rather than viewing this relationship as a cocreation of a new life between two people. People in cocreated marriages invest love into the relationship rather than the partner. Love R Us is a view of marriage that will rock your world if you fully engage in its principles.

In 1986, I moved from Springfield, Ohio, to Chicago to study at the Adler School of Professional Psychology. After I completed a master's degree at Wright State University, I pursued my doctorate at Adler. I chose this school primarily because of the work of Alfred Adler, a pioneer psychiatrist of the early 1900s.

Adler believed that all people address three major tasks in their search for fulfillment. Those three tasks are love, friendship, and work. Early in my training, I anchored those pursuits in my mind as central to understanding people. Dreikurs, in his book, *Fundamentals of Adlerian Psychology*, said, "The human community sets three tasks for every individual. They are: work, which means contributing to the welfare of others; friendship, which embraces social relationships with comrades and relatives; and love, which is the most intimate union."[1] Mysterious and elusive, yet constantly on our minds, at its height, love disrupts our focus from all other ambition.

If you went into a retail store to shop for *love* where would you look? If love had three primary qualities, which three would you look for? Would you walk around for a while scanning the possibilities? Would you look for fresh qualities or non-perishable ones? Maybe you would include qualities that you admire most in other relationships. I've observed in both life and clinical experience that the three key contributions to successfully loving our relationships are *respect, trust* and *humility.*

Loving the Us is like loving a person. The skills, gestures, and affection displayed between partners are also experienced in loving Us. The friendship a couple enjoys as a result of being Cooperative Is (CI) can be raised to a higher level by shifting focus so that the two individuals fall in love with their mutual investment—the Us.

The CI couple pours all their efforts into immediate demands rather than the long-term investment of loving the relationship, thereby missing the ultimate connection. It's like the difference between placing your hard-earned paycheck under the mattress or letting the bank hold it. Cash under the mattress may be safer, but the bank pays you dividends for you to risk leaving your money with them.

People who pour their love into another person will often be disappointed, but when they pour it into the relationship, they will usually receive a return. The CI marriage is fine companionship. Couples who function this way aren't necessarily dysfunctional or in need of repair. Two people cooperating and successfully negotiating a life together will certainly reap rewards. The Us connection allows for exponential growth and synergy, thus maximizing marriage beyond what a CI couple can enjoy.

Developing Us begins with a mindset change. The Chinese finger puzzle illustrates my point. My children recently won a finger puzzle at a carnival booth. The simple straw tube piqued their curiosity. I began the lesson by instructing each child to insert a finger in one end of the tube. Then I told them to try to get their fingers free. Their first instinct was to pull away from each other. Both of them jerked hard, then harder. Each time they did this, the tube strengthened its grip on their fingers. They giggled when they realized that all they had to do was to push their fingers closer together and the toy easily freed them.

Many couples try very hard to love each other only to find themselves trapped by the marriage itself. Loving the relationship provides a greater opportunity for a deep and lasting connection.

**Who Do We Love?**

Loving Us is a deviation from loving each other. Many relationship books focus on understanding the individuals, thereby making room for individual growth. Relationships are more than just "being there" for each other. Why do we need to be there for each other? Perhaps our purpose is to provide support, comfort, or companionship. There's nothing wrong with any of these needs, and I personally enjoy receiving these benefits from my own marriage. But why don't we think about being there for the relationship? The relationship is needy, too; and, like the individuals who are a part of it, needs attention to keep it vibrant and fresh.

I am friends with a couple who model the Us magic. When I think about them, I almost always think of *both* of them. They are a team. Each of them is different. They have separate likes and dislikes, but when we are with them, they are together. Their interactions focus on fairness to the marriage, rather than to each other. Once when they were preparing breakfast for guests, she suggested that one of them should prepare the pancakes while the other one served the food. He countered that they could both serve the food after the pancakes were done so their guests wouldn't have to wait. This may sound basic, but what is important is what is missing: arguing and the need to be right. They were both focused on presenting a united service that they genuinely wanted to deliver. I remember feeling appreciated by their hospitality and teamwork.

On the other hand, I've been in similar situations where just the opposite occurs. I recall one uncomfortable dinner, with a different couple, where sarcasm took over. The wife began making derogatory remarks and the husband was more than willing to fling them back. Comments like "If you would get off your butt and help, maybe I could get dinner on the table" or "You have to excuse my wife, she is cooking-impaired." In these situations, each person is trying to protect his or her individual image. Whether overt or subtle, the message is "every man for himself."

Criticism causes a division in teamwork. Jana and I have discovered this truth with money. She manages our money at home and work. She is an incredible organizer and record keeper. Only a few times in seventeen years has she bounced a check. If I were in charge, this would happen seventeen times per month. When she does make the mistake of not having the correct amount of funds, is it her fault? Is it my fault? Who is responsible? Before you answer too quickly, consider this. What if she bounced a mortgage check and the bank foreclosed on our house? What would that banker say if I said, "That was my wife's fault"? Would he let me continue living in the house as long as she left? Of course not! Who bounced the check? She did. Who is responsible for the bounced check? Both of us. The marriage relationship is responsible.

**Feed the Relationship**

As I said earlier, the three nutrients of a healthy relationship are *respect*, *trust*, and *humility*. The Love R Us connection feeds the relationship a daily diet of these three qualities. If I want a plant to grow, there are a few things that are absolutely necessary. You must have sunlight and water. Without these a plant will not grow. Without respect, trust, and humility a relationship will not grow. There may be various intrusions on the marriage—like weeds that impede plant growth, which need to be tended—however, all intrusions are secondary if the relationship has these three nutrients.

**Formula for Loving R Us**

*Practice rituals of respect for the relationship, moment to moment.*
*Deposit truckloads of Trust in the holes in your relationship.*
*Pour heaps of humility into the relationship continually while stirring up love.*

**Rituals of Respect**

While respect doesn't necessarily signify distance, it does require defined boundaries. According to Webster's, respect is "an act of giving special attention; high or special regard." Whom do you respect? When you hear a story about a man fighting off a shark to save his child, do you respect him? The heroes of the 9-11 tragedy were courageous under extreme stress. Do you respect them? Would you agree that Mother Teresa, a woman who committed her life to poverty, chastity, and caring for the castoffs of society, deserves respect? When we give people special regard, we treat them better. Likewise, when you respect each other, your marriage will reap multiple benefits.

We behave differently with famous people. People who ride in limousines, hold public positions, or wear the mantle of Hollywood fame receive more respect from us than the average waiter or clerk. Our values about wealth, intellect, and beauty guide our beliefs about those we esteem.

Billy Graham had just finished a tour of the Florida East Coast and was taking a limousine to the airport. Having never driven a limo, he asked the chauffeur if he could drive for a while. Well, the chauffeur didn't have much of a choice, so he got in the back of the limo, and Billy took the wheel.

*He turned onto I-95 and accelerated to about 90 mph. WHAM! The blue lights of the State Highway Patrol flashed in his rearview mirror. He pulled over, and a trooper came to his window. When the trooper saw who it was, he said, "Just a minute, please, I need to call in."*

*The trooper radioed in and asked for the chief. He said, "I have a REALLY important person pulled over and I need to know what to do." The chief replied, "Who is it, not Ted Kennedy again?" The trooper said, "No, even more important." "It isn't Governor Jeb Bush, is it?" asked the chief. "No, even more important." "Well, who in the WORLD is it?" screamed the chief. The trooper responded, "I don't know for sure, but I think it might be Jesus, because his chauffeur is Billy Graham!"*

When you first started dating your mate, did you treat her like a famous person? Respect is usually evident on the first few dates. You were probably polite and generous with your partner. Communications were thoughtful and sensitive because you wanted to express the utmost respect. But once couples marry, a terrible thing happens. We take ownership, let down our hair, and completely forget those wonderful courting techniques. Most people desire respect. From the skinny little guy fighting for his right to play ball to the lofty speeches of Martin Luther King Jr., respect is demanded and deserved by all races, genders, and religions. Husbands and wives are no different. In fact, the need for esteem between two people is no greater in any relationship than for couples. The successful marriage relationship provides a model for the ultimate respect needed to overcome individual differences of any social group. Respect would prevent many divorces, absentee spouses, and domestic violence.

I can't imagine being married to someone I don't respect. To marry a person you don't respect is a direct reflection of your own self-worth. Jana is my favorite person in the whole world. I hold her in high regard. Why would I allow my relationship to falter because of a respect issue with her? Perhaps our confusion begins with the origin of respect. Do we earn it first, or is it given freely? Do we give it freely, or must it be earned from us?

In real life, you find yourselves partnered with people who have moral breakdowns, addictions, mental illnesses, and many other undesirable problems. This is no fairy tale. Just because you know your partner with all his or her flaws, doesn't mean respect must fly out the window. No matter how unusual a relationship is, it will thrive on mutual respect. When respect disappears, the potential for love has been compromised.

Rituals of respect can be given to the relationship just like you would put fuel in a car. It may be easy or unimaginable, but making frequent fill-ups is what relationships need to keep going. When you believe your partner doesn't deserve respect, look in the mirror and ask yourself if you have done what you need to do to earn respect. The answer will most likely be no. A good friend of mine often says, "Give 'em what they need, not what they deserve." They need what you hope you will get from them: grace.

**Truckloads of Trust**

*Over the years, an old dog became a trapper's best friend. Living in a remote forest at the northern edge of Canada didn't offer him much chance for friends. Every few days he and his dog would go off to check traps. He sold his pelts at a trading post for necessities. It was a simple life.*

*The two shared each other's company for more than ten years. The dog loved the man, and often protected him from wild animals in the rough country.*

*One trip to town changed everything. A woman had taken over the trading post and she and the trapper hit it off. He found himself making more frequent trips into town.*

*They wed in the spring and she moved to the trapper's cabin. Their first child was due the following winter and the trapper's wife moved back to town to give birth, but tragedy followed. The wife died in childbirth, leaving the care of a new daughter to the trapper. He faced the challenge of raising a child while sustaining their existence. Now, he often left the dog behind to guard the child while he traveled alone to check his traps. He trusted his dog with the sleeping baby knowing the beloved pet would protect her from danger. One day, tragedy visited this small family once again.*

*Returning home early one morning, the trapper came over the last hill to see the front door of the cabin pushed open. With his heart pounding wildly, the trapper thrust aside his pelts and hurried to the cabin to verify his daughter's safety.*

*As he entered the cabin, his worst fears were confirmed. The baby's cradle was covered in a blood-drenched blanket. He noticed from the corner of his eye that his dog cowered in one corner, his nose bloody.*

*In a moment of rage, screaming epithets at the murderous dog, the man cocked his rifle and almost shot the dog. His yelling woke the baby, who began to cry. Startled by this unexpected turn, he threw back the bloody blanket to see the daughter unharmed.*

*As he inspected his daughter's little body for the source of blood, he noticed a dead bobcat lying on the cabin floor behind the crib. In a heartbreaking moment of understanding, he realized that he almost killed his precious dog before perceiving what really happened.*

Hasty conclusions and impulsive rage can destroy the beautiful trust between two people. The marriage relationship can potentially provide the same bond that the trapper and his dog enjoyed. Life events may distract partners from one another, but each new life experience—when faced together—is an opportunity to vault to a deeper level of trust. Trust is wonderful. We develop trust as we share our life. We slowly risk our valued treasures with our partner. Yet, it's almost as if we have a built-in instinct to blame the ones we love when things go wrong. I have found that couples often explode at each other the moment their lives take a bad turn. This happens even with clear evidence that the partner is not at fault.

When trust is exploited, the trust-giver often removes it too soon. We all need space to be forgiven and understood. Trust is difficult to rebuild after a violation, and emotional vulnerability, anger, and denial often cloud the real issues that must be addressed to heal the relationship. Couples should assess the offender's action to discover what went wrong. Infidelity plays large in trust destruction. Infidelity is a violation that points to significant relationship problems in need of repair. To regain trust, the victim must avoid hasty conclusions and impulsive actions. Trust is a fluid attribute that increases and decreases over time. During times of low trust, the relationship experiences great stress. Trust must be stored up by the truckloads during the strong times of any relationship to weather the storms that come. Terry Hargrave, author of *The Essential Humility of Marriage*, suggests, "The key element of trust is the ability to give freely to another believing that the other will responsibly and reliably give back."[2] This allows the relationship to move forward toward maturity and balance.

**Heaps of Humility**

In a great marriage, each partner is able to surrender to the relationship with heaps of humility. Humility is evidenced by the absence of control. A humble person first recognizes his own shortcomings. The focus on our own flaws deters us from the need to point out those of our partner. A humble spouse seeks to do right rather than pressuring the partner to do right. Many religions focus on the process of humility. Words like submission, long suffering, patience, kindness, and gentleness describe humble loving. Public opinion suggests that humility equals low self-esteem. That to be humble is to be a doormat. That if you aren't happy in your marriage, you should just get out. Divorce rates affirm the recent social belief that if you're not getting your own needs met, you should end the marriage. Humility, however, paves the way for a two-way street. True humility does not include being a wimpy doormat to your spouse. Nevertheless, humility is often viewed as a weakness in our culture. We champion winners over team players. We value money over love, and things over people.

Conversely, mutual humility produces soft, malleable soil that prospers a relationship. When two people come together with a realistic vision of themselves and each other, they can better prepare and plan for their life together. Hargrave suggests, "The heart of an Us is not that I sacrifice my individuality for my wife, but that I willingly give a part of who I am for the sake of the relationship."[3] Humility cannot be given sparingly when growing a relationship of unity and collaboration.

For two things to merge into one, there has to be a mutual surrender. Two rigid metals will not be joined until they are reduced to soft metal through heat. Flames soften the metal to produce a new, stronger compound. Likewise, a couple's love can be melted into a powerful joining after humility softens both. You can never have enough humility to keep the flames hot and the metal soft. Thus these powerful words were weaved into the marriage vow: "What God has joined together, let no man put asunder."

"There are two kinds of sparks, the one that goes off without a hitch like a match, but it burns quickly. The other is the kind that needs time, but when the flame strikes…it's eternal, don't forget that." —*Timothy Oliveira*

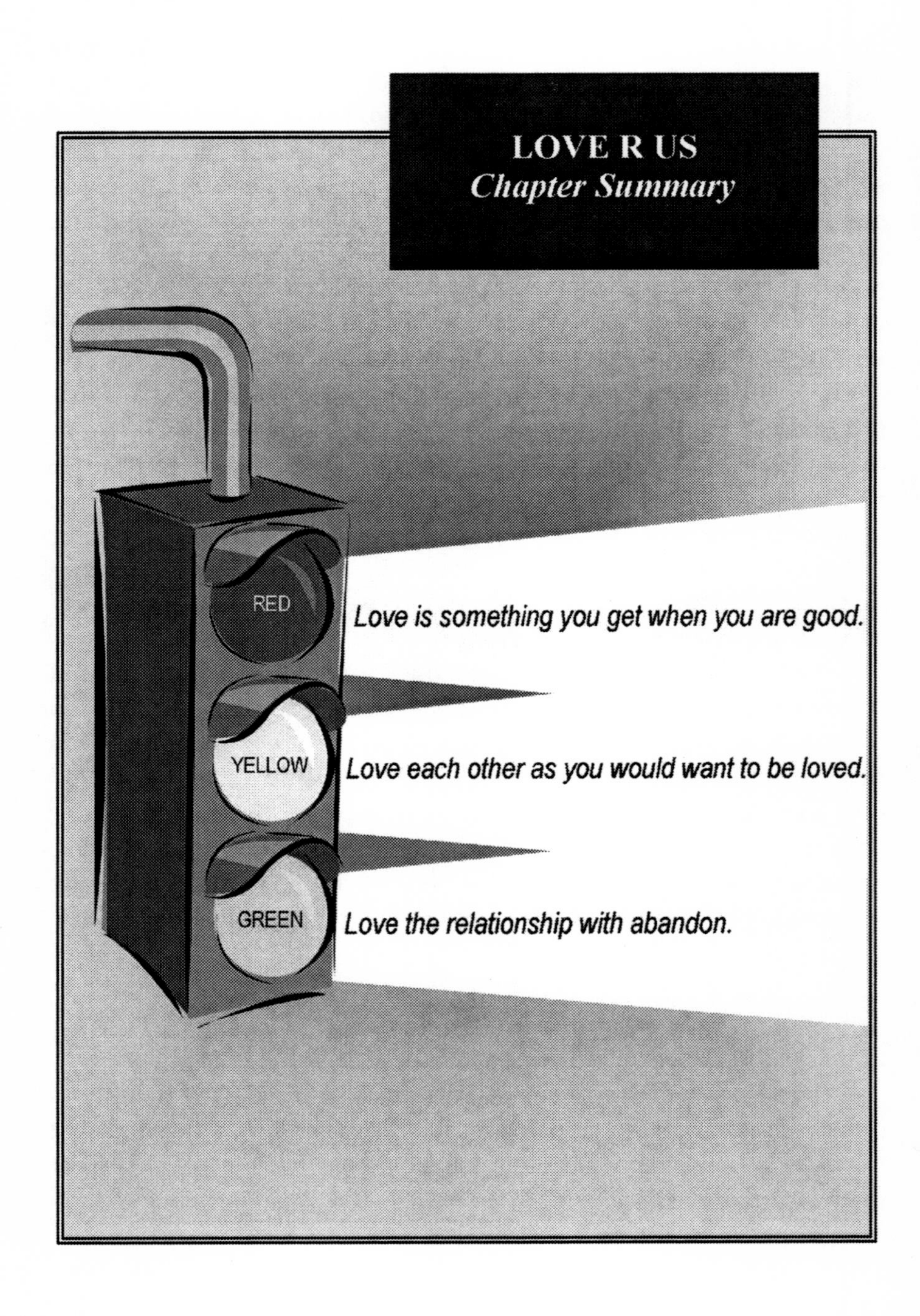
LOVE R US
Chapter Summary
RED
Love is something you get when you are good.
YELLOW
Love each other as you would want to be loved.
GREEN
Love the relationship with abandon.

*Chapter Eight*

# Sex From the Us Position

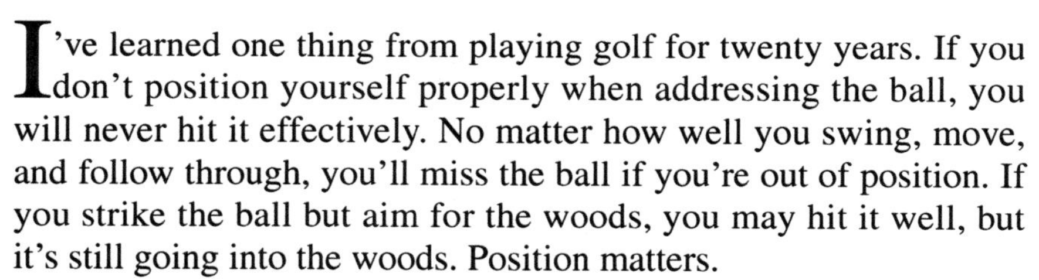

I've learned one thing from playing golf for twenty years. If you don't position yourself properly when addressing the ball, you will never hit it effectively. No matter how well you swing, move, and follow through, you'll miss the ball if you're out of position. If you strike the ball but aim for the woods, you may hit it well, but it's still going into the woods. Position matters.

Like golf, a healthy sex life begins with proper positioning. I want to share with you three relational positions and explain their usefulness. Throughout this book I have referred to three styles of marriage. I believe these same three styles make a clear illustration for sexual interaction. So I will be discussing sex from the Me position, Fee position, and the We position.

I heard an illustration that expresses my thoughts on sex and marriage. The sexual relationship is comparable to mountain climbing. Imagine you're climbing a mountain with two friends, hoping to reach the summit. You've determined that it would take three days to get there. During the first day you've labored, sacrificed, and navigated your way through difficult terrain as a team. You are exhausted, dazed, and excited. On the second day you notice some commotion ahead of you. When you get to the source of the noise, you realize two people have been dropped off by plane and are appearing to join you on the climb. You wonder how they could coordinate that sort of drop off. Being tired from the first day, you realize why they did it. On the third, after putting in many hours, you realize you'll make it to the summit. What a rush!

Suddenly, the whacking thunder of helicopter blades forces your eyes skyward. You look up as the helicopter lands one hundred yards away. Two other climbers jump from the aircraft and join you in your climb. When you reach the top, you pause, exhilarated, to enjoy the view and relish your accomplishment. You notice the two late arrivals doing the same. Are they experiencing the same euphoria? Of course not! They didn't have the experiences you had to get there. The first team to join you will have some perspective, but the last team will have only the "moment." They took a shortcut to the summit.

Similarly, couples often want the "peak experience" without making the climb. Some quit climbing because it feels like too much work. Others devote the time and expend the energy required to take the hill enjoying the challenges, discoveries, and delights along the way.

I observe many different variations of the three positions in my work with couples. I've concluded that most couples rarely experience sex from a truly united relational position.

"Writing is like making love. Don't worry about the orgasm, just concentrate on the process." *—Isabel Allende*

**Me Sex**

Obviously, this is the insatiable preoccupation with one person's sexual needs. The Me sex couple agree to allow sex to be used by one individual as a sort of extra perk in trade for succumbing to marriage. It isn't something to pay for or work for; it's just part of the deal. It's like staying in a hotel with a free continental breakfast. Options for breakfast are often limited to old coffee, hard bagels, and some fruit that looks like it's been run through a dishwasher. If you're in a hurry, you grab something and go. That's what Me sex is like. You know it's not that great, but you take it and run.

This type of sex promotes ultra-independence and self-directedness. The concept of mutually gratifying each other's needs never occurs. Sex from this position at best maintains status quo while providing spikes of personal pleasure for one member of the team.

One husband stuck in this arrangement was surprised by his wife's disappointment with their sex life. He was content stealing sex from the marriage because his needs were met. She would remain a passive participant during sex. He was aware that she wasn't into it, but he figured that was *her* problem. No matter how much they fought, ignored each other, or hurt each other emotionally, he still expected sex.

Until she began healing her own wounds, she didn't realize how this damaged both her and the relationship. Once in awhile both parties may be served by a Me sex arrangement. The old movie *Baby Boom* shows a married couple reading in bed together. One beckons the other with a smile and the other responds. The camera zooms in on the clock, showing 10:32 p.m. In the next scene, the couple is again sitting up in bed reading, and the clock shows 10:38 p.m. They are both smiling.

When sex is nothing more than a biological function for both partners, then the Me sex approach can be functional. More often than not, however, Me sex serves only one partner. It occurs most often when laziness or disrespect lead to lack of communication and intimacy in a relationship. I personally do not recommend this kind of arrangement be used too often because of the lack of relational connection. Nevertheless, I listed what I notice as possible positive and negative outcomes from Me sex.

| Possible Useful Functions | Possible Destructive Outcomes |
| --- | --- |
| Physical release | Interpersonal distance |
| Personal pleasure | Bitterness on the giver's part |
| Stress reduction | Negates unity |
| Can serve adequately for a "quickie" | Promotes selfishness |

"Sex and golf are the two things you can enjoy even if you're not good at them." —*Kevin Costner, Tin Cup*

**Fee Sex**

This is the most common arrangement I have found among married couples, and it is cooperative. Both partners comprehend that sex is necessary to marriage and they are attracted to each other. Both partners negotiate their needs fairly. Give to get—get to give. I've often played this game with my wife. She requests help with some project, and I smile and agree with the stipulation that she help me with "my little project" (eyebrows bobbing like a pogo stick). This playful interaction is probably common and can be very positive for the marriage relationship. You make a date with each other, say all the right things, create a safe emotional environment, and play to one another's preferences.

I have been teaching the three T-skills of sexual programming for more than ten years. I borrowed my idea for T-skills from the joke that men only hope for sex on days that begin with T: Tuesday, Thursday, today, tomorrow, T-aturday and T-unday. The three T's are *tenderness*, *touching*, and *telling*.

***Tenderness***

Tenderness skills include affection, gentleness, and romance. A moment of tenderness can start the "engines" all by themselves. When couples are intimate, they are usually involved in softer more sensitive exchanges. I encourage couples who want regular healthy sexual encounters to build these times into the daily routine. As Leman's book title suggests, sex begins in the kitchen. Moment by moment, affirmations and glances explode into magical experiences when genuinely expressed. This is perhaps the most necessary, yet neglected relational skill.

A few years ago I held a marriage retreat that focused primarily on the issue of romance. I titled the retreat "A Romantic Getaway" and called participants Romantic Rascals. The goal of the weekend was to rekindle tenderness and closeness between the couples. All the couples admitted sorely lacking in this area of their marriage and found the weekend very helpful. When tenderness is practiced, the likelihood increases for positive sexual interaction. Tenderness may be the best aphrodisiac there is for most women. Although men may not ask for these emotional strokes, they often enjoy receiving them just as much as women.

***Touching***

The second T-skill is touching. Mounting evidence in social research identifies a desperate need by humans to be touched. Unfortunately, men most often get touched through competition, fighting, or during sex. Hence, men are not routinely going to touch their wives without that goal-orientation rearing its head. Men enjoy being touched, but their early conditioning taught them that softness is for girls. Additionally, because men are taught not to express a soft side, they may feel awkward touching other men. Therefore they tend to reserve touch only for sexual activity. Women learn to avoid touching their husbands, fearing the need to proffer sex immediately. By stepping around this "unspoken contract," women often sacrifice the touch they so keenly desire.

I teach couples to touch each other in a variety of non-sexual situations. Women want touch without sexual pressure because it makes them feel valued and appreciated in ways that reinforce them as women rather than objects. Hugging, handholding, and stroking are a great start to practicing touching skills. Make sure this touching does not lead to sex during your early trials.

***Telling***

Telling is the third of the T-skills. Communication is obviously important for any type of relationship. To have a successful sexual relationship, talking is equally important. There seems to be a shortage of words when it comes to sexual desires. Most couples resort to nonverbal signals and habitual patterns to express desire. Researchers are finding that men and women don't understand their partner's sexuality and therefore need to learn each other's "language" before positive sexual communication can occur. The telling skill aids in this learning process. Think of it as advanced Show and Tell.

Under the covers after the lights are out, what can you learn? You're married! Lose your inhibitions and begin some exploration with the lights on. Candlelight is perfect. Once you begin showing yourself to your partner, tell them everything you know about your precious treasures. This myth that your partner should know what you like if he "knows" you is a lie. Another myth is that you'll learn everything you need to know about the opposite sex from your friends. All men and women are not interchangeable. This partner of yours has no match. Don't refer to outside sources to teach you what your partner can tell you. Open, honest telling can be fun and extremely educational. One couple I worked with said it was like learning about each other all over again. They had been married for twelve years and never discussed some of the finer details of their sexual preferences. Men usually do not enjoy marital counseling until I start assigning sex homework. For some unknown reason I suddenly become a smart guy.

The Fee sex arrangement is built on the understanding that if we learn as much as we can about each other and cooperate, we can have a great sex life. Of course the payoff is that we get something for our effort. I have heard of trading sex for duties, money, trips, babysitting—you name it. In the Cooperative I marriage, sex is just another way to show your partner you are willing to contribute to his or her welfare.

Sex in this arrangement will usually be motivated by the other person's needs. I'll scratch your back if you scratch mine. This works very well for couples until one decides not to cooperate. The perfect arrangement will be upset by the infamous headache, tiredness, or late work. When cooperation is perceived to be ended, selfishness takes a front seat. This "withholding" cycle can last for hours, days, weeks, or even months. The most common breakdown occurs when the woman is not interested in sex as often as her partner. This is perceived as an unwillingness to share in the marriage games, or worse, as a personal insult. The man may avoid some of his household duties in retaliation, and the battle is on.

Fee sex arrangements are great when everyone cooperates, but terrible when communications break down. Most couples operating at this level do enjoy a very nice sex life. But because cooperative couples don't invest in the relationship, any upset—illness, childbirth, job loss, or boredom—decreases flexibility.

Fee sex is based on predictability, and life is anything but predictable. In my marriage, unusual circumstances are normal and predictable situations are rare.

"Some things are better than sex, and some are worse, but there's nothing exactly like it." —*W.C. Fields*

**We Sex**

We sex, or sex from the Us position, is the Super Bowl of sexual experiences. Just as in football, most teams can't make it every year. Likewise, this sexual connection isn't always possible. Nevertheless, it is worth addressing our ultimate goal. In our climbing story, you would be the couple who work together for three days, struggling against the obstacles to reach that mountain peak. You are both equally invested in reaching the top because being there together means you accomplished it for the team, not for individual gain. You sit at the top together and say, "We did it!" Not, "You greatly helped me achieve this goal. Thanks a lot."

We sex is always focused on Us needs, not individual needs. The common consensus is that what is good for Us is good for me. Anything short of good for Us is unacceptable.

The good news is that We sex requires lots of practice, the bad news is that it also requires lots of maturity. Sex for the relationship requires very different things than selfish sex (or selfish withholding). For instance, you may enjoy having sex on the beach at midnight, but We may not be up for that. You have to understand the nature of We in order to reconcile your private fantasies with We sex. Me sex might demand the activity, and Fee sex might deal for it. We sex is not interested in deals because needs and desires change.

During sex from the Us position, partners enjoy sex for the

relationship's sake. Hargrove suggests, "Sex is one of the few activities in which we consciously lose control of ourselves with another person. This is truly a golden highway—I give to my beloved in such a complete way that I lose part of myself in the process. And it is not a painful loss, but a loss that culminates in a blissful 'ahhh.' " [1] At that moment, we are suspended in an unearthly state that catapults the relationship to deeper connections, or drives us to replicate the experience compulsively for selfish gain. How do couples make the appropriate shift? This shift has to be intentional, mindful, and developed together.

Building a We sex arrangement requires an Us marriage style. Examples I have used in previous chapters fit usefully in this chapter. With sex there are unique hurdles to jump. The first hurdle is experiencing sex as a result of love, rather than finding love through sex. The We sex partners reciprocate tenderness, touching, and telling regularly and also happen to enjoy great sex from time to time. Their emphasis is on daily cultivating that loving connection.

When sex occurs spontaneously from loving actions and emotional connections, the experience is unusually meaningful. Let's say you and your spouse have spent the weekend in loving rhythm. You've shared duties, hugs, and several relational investment moments. Except for a few tasks and errands separating you, you've been touching, laughing, and playing together all weekend. You're both in the kitchen fixing dinner and it hits you. You become overwhelmed with passion and barely make it to the couch. There is no bickering, no negotiating, and lots of laughter. Has it ever happened to you? When the relationship is ready for a sexual experience, it rings the bell and both partners respond with equal abandon.

On the other hand, you are probably familiar with the other version of this same scenario. You do separate household duties cordially all weekend. You communicate what you're doing and where you're going but really don't spend much of the weekend together. It's a productive (cooperative) weekend and both partners feel they have used their time wisely.

You are in the kitchen fixing dinner and you say to your spouse, "It's been a great weekend. Why don't we top it off by fooling around before dinner?" Your spouse responds, "Well, let's get dinner, and then see from there." At this point you are pumped. You didn't get instant sex, but it's a good bet you'll get some soon. After dinner, as she begins to clean up, she complains that she is tired. You quickly offer to clean up while she rests. You want nothing to spoil your chances.

Your partner watches a movie while you clean up. This is going to be good. You've planned a fantasy session in your head. As you join her on the couch, she asks, "Can we snuggle for awhile?" You do it. The promise for more is still there. You both enjoy the snuggling until she makes the dreaded suggestion, "Why don't we just cuddle tonight, and we can be together tomorrow. I'm tired and want to finish the movie."

You're highly disappointed but agree, for now. Regardless if you have sex or not that night, the relationship does not demand lovemaking. In this situation, you are interested, but your spouse isn't. This scenario is common. The best you can hope for is a Fee sex arrangement.

What could have made a difference? If you reflected back on the weekend you might remember your spouse asking you to help her in the basement. Or you might remember that back rub you passed up when you were on your way out the door. Maybe you thought about cleaning up the dishes before you went to bed Saturday night, but you were too tired. Were there times when a hug would have spoken more clearly than your words? Each time you have a chance to connect, you can have a relational investment moment (RIM). The RIMs can add up quickly during the week and pay dividends when you need them most.

These small investments cannot be replaced. They aren't required; but they feed the relationship, which builds the foundation for great We sex. A man often desires sex any time, anywhere, anyhow. Women are more selective. The relationship balances out these two extremes when both partners deposit consistent investments toward the relationship. Relational deposits may not be individually convenient, yet they will pay double the dividends in those We sex moments.

The second hurdle is discovering that frequency and variety of sexual encounters don't determine quality. Sex from the Us position may not happen as often, but when it does, deep and intimate connections are made. With plentiful and varying information about frequency of sex, how can a couple determine what is normal? Every couple is creating their own unique relationship, so comparisons can debilitate the partnership. I have worked with couples who have sex every day, yet have rarely experienced a dynamic connection. They sacrifice quality for quantity.

When a couple chooses quantity over quality in their sexual patterns, they may be disappointed. Great physical experiences don't guarantee an Us connection. Often, partners anxiously attempt to fill emotional and relational emptiness by having sex more frequently. This temporary fix never brings partners closer to the payoff of lifetime intimacy.

The last hurdle couples must clear is adjusting to the curveballs of life. Any couple married for more than a month knows about intrusions, distractions, and physical limitations in their sex life. In our first year of marriage, Jana and I gladly invited her sister to live with us while preparing for her own marriage. She was like a sister to me and was a joy to have around. However, this proved to be an unexpected distraction for our budding sexual relationship. I was perfectly willing to ignore her sister's presence, but Jana was more inhibited.

When children came along, our sex life didn't ring as often. I remember wondering if things would ever be exciting again. Like most relational distractions, this too was temporary. However, many couples do not adapt to these transitional issues as well as others. Illness, injury, and emotional depletion are all normal life nuisances. If the relationship is nurtured daily, it will eventually call for sex. The proper balance of assertiveness and surrender to the relationship maintains a healthy sexual partnership.

"We make love every night, and have sex occasionally."
—*Quote from a sexually satisfied couple*

## Maintaining Your Sex Life

About eighteen years ago, I had a terrible toothache. The pain was manageable at first, so I just put up with it. Over the course of the ensuing weeks and months, I became sicker and sicker. I seemed to be suffering from depression. I was sluggish and despondent. A good friend was getting married and I was his best man. I drove around with him the day before the wedding complaining of this awful toothache. He was annoyed with my refusal to get help. After the wedding, I continued to ignore the increasing pain by gulping pain relievers daily. One night, I woke in excruciating pain and paced around my apartment for a couple of hours. Embarrassed but humbled, I woke my wife and admitted I was in trouble. I went to the dentist without an appointment that next morning, determined to stay until the source of pain was identified. Within a few hours, I was getting a root canal. Later, the doctor informed me I could have prevented months of suffering and stress to my health if I had come in when the pain started. Instead, the infection depleted my immune system and caused fatigue and depression in addition to the intense pain.

Couples often approach small sexual problems in marriage the way I did my toothache. Most relational disasters could be avoided with a little prevention early on like going to a seminar, reading a book, or visiting a marriage counselor. Lack of healthy sexual communication and refusal to deal with sexual conflict are the two most common culprits of declined sexual activity. Sexless marriages are equally as damaging as an emotionless marriages or marriages lacking loyalty.

Sex is an extremely important connection that promotes a healthy marriage. You and your spouse can experience a fun-filled, hopelessly romantic, warmly intimate sex life. By using the three styles of sexual interaction as your guide, you can enjoy a balance of all three experiences. I suggest you decide together what percentage of sex time you would like to devote to each style. I recommended the balance of time spent to be around; 20 percent toward *Me sex*, 40 percent toward *Fee sex*, and 40 percent toward *We sex*. Using this as your guide, you can allow for a variety of sexual experiences while attempting to weed out unwanted misunderstandings and confusion.

When relationally positioned, thoughtfully balanced, and passionately expressed, sex is a wonderful thing.

"Think of how God can reveal himself to you within your marriage through the gift of sexual pleasure." —*Gary Thomas,* Sacred Marriage

SEX FROM THE US
POSITION
Chapter Summary
RED
Great sex means I am happy.
YELLOW
Great sex means we are happy.
GREEN
Great sex means the relationship is happy.

*Chapter Nine*

# Soul Mates

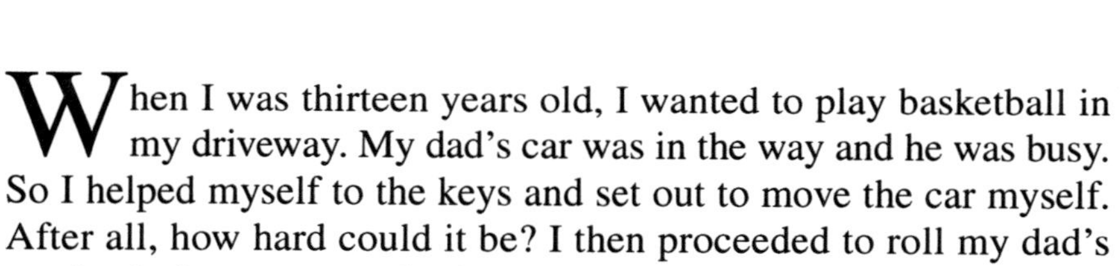

When I was thirteen years old, I wanted to play basketball in my driveway. My dad's car was in the way and he was busy. So I helped myself to the keys and set out to move the car myself. After all, how hard could it be? I then proceeded to roll my dad's car back into my mother's car. I didn't hit it directly; it just sideswiped her car from front to end. The last thing I wanted to do was to go inside and report what I had done. I avoided going inside for hours. This same feeling occurred when I began writing this chapter. I was avoiding it. In fact, I was tempted to leave this chapter out of the book. I considered referring you to a few well-written books on this subject, relieving me of the challenge.

God did not let me off the hook so easily. I feel pressed to confess my own battle, to comfort readers in the knowledge that Christ loves us despite our struggles and failures. There are plenty of how-to books on spiritual intimacy. But there are no rules, formulas, or behaviors to lead couples to find Christ in their marriage. Each couple is left to discover God in their own way. Today, I observe couples asking questions about and wanting to become soul mates. It is my conviction that the deepest soul connection comes from a Christ-centered, Holy Spirit–guided,

God-fearing marriage.

Because the soul is central to all human behavior, I believe it is the most important connection a couple can make. How a person acts, thinks, and feels is based on belief. For example, the belief that Christ is director and Savior of our lives changes how we choose, love, and respond to others.

Regardless how we choose to define it, the soul is obviously an important key to our meaningful relationships. At the core of the soul are the mysterious questions about our creator and our kinship with Him. Regardless of religion or philosophy, how couples embrace their belief in the supernatural is significant to the marriage.

As soon as couples begin to share their core beliefs, family-of-origin issues crop up divisively. Most people attain their beliefs in God in childhood. Often, the religious doctrines we're raised with permeate our lives. I've worked with people who either reject God based on their early training or embrace God because of it. Our interpretations of those "teaching moments" shape our thinking about God. Unless mates share an identical family –of origin, partners will need to respectfully accept and share their differences. When you make a deep connection with your mate, some beliefs are likely to be challenged.

Jana and I had a special spiritual connection from the beginning of our relationship. Our first date was at church. We started praying together as soon as I convinced her to date me exclusively. (That took some time!) My favorite wedding picture shows us kneeling in prayer encircled by our parents, the maid of honor and the best man. This was how we designed our marriage; with Christ at the center and a safety net of loved ones surrounding us in prayer. Everyone doesn't start out in marriage this way. The miracle is that couples can come to God at any point in their relationship and He will strengthen their foundations and make their marriages new.

Although we started out Christ-centered, Jana and I are still discovering new aspects of our soul journey. In trying to live our day-to-day lives, it is easy to stray from this journey. I am encouraged by a quote from John Ortberg in his book *The Life You've Always Wanted*: "The truth is that the term spiritual life is simply a way of referring to one's life—every moment and facet of it—from

God's perspective. Another way of saying it is this: God is not interested in your 'spiritual life.' God is just interested in your life."[1]

In the same way, *God is not interested in a spiritual marriage—He's interested in your marriage.* He wants to be active in your lives beyond an occasional bed-time prayer. When I am talking to my wife about how to raise our children we are engaged in spiritual development. He desires to be a part of our communication, closeness, and commitment to each other. He created man and wife to partner with him in all aspects of their relationship. Think of a Christ-centered marriage as having a hub for all marriage activity. The hub serves as the lifeline to the variety of relationship tasks. Whether you are working on communication, conflicts, or intimacy, all activities are spiritually developing the relationship. I am envisioning that developing a Christ-centered hub leads couples in making soul-to-soul connections on multiple levels.

**From Stories to Relationships**

I became interested in knowing God through childhood Bible stories that were repeated like breathing in my home. I remember stories of David and Goliath, Joseph and his brothers, Jonah and the whale, and the birth, life, and death of Jesus. I became attached to these colorful Bible characters and their battles for God.

In high school, I began exploring my own views about God. Since college, I have been on a journey to know Christ in a more personal way. In a theology class I took a few years ago, I was introduced to various approaches to knowing God. One way to understand God is through analogies. This is common to human relationships as well. Since we have no way of knowing God entirely, we rely on stories about God's relationships to others. We must be cautious that our ideas about God don't replace a relationship with Him.

God reveals himself to us as we create ideas about our experience with God and share them through analogy. But talking *about* God is not the same as talking *to* Him. Likewise, couples have a tendency to focus on their ideas about one another, even when they become outdated. For example, a husband assumes his wife is not interested in his work because she tends to be unresponsive when he talks about it. As she comes to know him and the value he holds in his job, she develops more interest in it. If he's not paying attention, he'll take the idea "she isn't interested in my job" and turn it into a belief about her.

The five *marital tasks* outlined in this book could be helpful in establishing a soul connection. When *closeness* combines with *commitment* and *communication*, the relationship begins to jell. When you work out *compatibility* issues and *cooperate* with each other, your home becomes a safe harbor for loving, caring, and sharing.

I was coaching a premarital couple who was exploring the possibility of a long-term relationship. This would be a second marriage for both of them, and they wanted a deeper more meaningful relationship this time. As they began to connect, they both questioned their core values about their careers and intimacy. As the relationship began to form, they struggled with their *compatibility* differences. They engaged in *closeness* through sharing daily experiences, yet struggled with the value of their growing emotional connection. The risks were huge, and the couple's personal revelations scared them. Their *communication* task was being challenged throughout the courtship and continued while attempting to proceed with relationship coaching. They ultimately learned to respect each other's perspectives. The task of *cooperation* was a challenge, yet they struggled enough to appreciate the necessity of working as a team. They both had opportunities to be disloyal, but they backed each other up. The final issue of *commitment* was resolved during our coaching when they set a date for their wedding. Of course, they will have difficult times when they will have to share ugly secrets to gain trust. Like the first big surprise, just weeks before the wedding date, that she had been unfaithful in her previous marriage. This love has to be put into motion, not just emotion. They will struggle to be happy together, yet the struggle may birth the best part of how they become soul mates.

**Spiritual Sweet Spot**

Many couples are spiritually gasping to survive, let alone preparing for Christ to lead them to the "spiritual sweet spot." This is the spot where individuals reserve space for the spiritual connection to take root. I find deep spiritual intimacy rare among most Christian couples for two reasons. First, they are struggling just to spend quality time with God themselves. Second, most couples are not close enough to each other to allow the space for spiritual growth.

Spiritual intimacy cannot develop any more than emotional intimacy. When couples do not grow together, they are likely to grow apart. In faith communities, couples tend to serve in separate programs—she gets involved in women's ministry and he gets involved in sports and men's Bible studies. If things go well, they both grow spiritually by investing in their ministry areas. Occasionally they worship together, but only when they're both free of job assignments. They rarely discuss their spiritual growth, and prayer is often limited to quickies at dinner and bedtime. Their faith gives them strength yet they clearly miss something. It's frustrating to watch churches set up conflicting programs that inadvertently prevent couples from intimate spiritual experiences. I've served three times as a staff pastor and became conscious of how vulnerable church leaders' marriages are to this loss. Couples in leadership are often separated in their faith community "work place." They must be disciplined at building a safe haven in their spiritual connection. God in Us demands that the couple build a powerful relationship.

When a couple marries, they commit to leaving their previous family identities, cleaving to each other and weaving a "one" relationship. Allander and Longman, authors of *Intimate Allies*, believe, "The goal of marriage is twofold: To reveal the glory of God and to enhance the glory of one's spouse."[2] Therefore, we have only two options, to glorify or to degrade our partner. To glorify our spouse suggests we view each other as mysterious and glorious children of God. In doing this, we reflect the image of God in each other. To demean, criticize, ignore, control, or verbally assault a spouse would degrade our partner's glory and our own.

Weaving a marriage relationship is both exciting and difficult. When Christ is the focal point for values, principles, and service, it eases the process significantly. If Christ is Lord of your life, why not allow Him to lead your marriage? Merge your interests, dreams, and goals by asking Him to direct your path. Picture a couple looking upward toward God for guidance, eyes drawn toward one goal, connected to each other at the apex. With God in the middle, His position is at the top of a triangle, each corner anchored at the base by husband and wife. As each partner looks and moves upward toward God, they not only draw a line to God, they also close the gap between themselves. In short, God is the Us in marriage. He waits patiently for couples to surrender to a relationship centered in Him and designed by His love and wisdom.

**Seeds to Soul**

Soul connections differ from marriage improvement tools. Soul connections are about discovering God in your partner or others. In developing soul connections in my own life and marriage, I've benefited from three concepts author Larry Crabb outlines in his book, *The Safest Place on Earth.*[3] I'll use the metaphor of planting seeds as a way to describe the three concepts of *brokenness*, *holiness,* and *openness*. When nurtured, these three seeds allow your marriage to experience spiritual growth and prepare you for spiritual intimacy.

***The Seed of Brokenness***

The first seed of brokenness is accepting that you alone can't make your marriage more spiritual. Being a broken and willing vessel allows God to work in you and your relationship. No matter how often we attend church, pray, or call on the sick, we cannot create a spiritual moment. I remember having a need to connect to His Spirit one night because I couldn't sleep. I went out for a drive and found myself talking to God in the church parking lot where I attended. I had a church key so I let myself in and went down to the front of the sanctuary. I lay down on my back, looked up at the stained glass window, and prayed for God to meet with me. I was hungry for a "spiritual experience." I laid there for two hours asking God to meet with me. Nothing happened, I got tired and went home.

I shared this experience with my accountability group, and they laughed at my obvious attempt to summon the Holy Spirit. My discovery was simple. You can't conjure up the Holy Spirit because you can't sleep. I was looking to use God for my own entertainment, like finding a TV show to watch when I am bored. I don't regret going to the church because I had some much needed quiet time. Nevertheless, I shouldn't have been disappointed when God didn't show up in his Superman suit and throw me some fireballs. It also afforded me the realization, again, that I must remain broken before God to sense His presence.

I have talked to couples who "feel" nothing when they pray or when they talk about God. They pray for help from God and don't seem to be getting answers. Our "instant-fix" thinking places God in some sort of repairman category and we become angry when he doesn't show up on call. Communicating with God requires great patience and faith. He is faithful and His timing is perfect. We shouldn't humanize God by expecting him to respond instantly to our fears and blunders.

In college, while in a group setting, a few friends and I inadvertently began to open up. Our sharing of confessions, dreams, and insecurities led to a deep connection. Although it was unplanned, it was not undirected. Since then, those bonds have stood the test of time and distance. My relationships with these men continue to demonstrate extraordinary intimacy. We may not talk for months, yet we can come back to that bond within moments. This connection is deeper than shared experiences and fond memories. It's based on honesty, vulnerability, and *brokenness*.

Getting spiritual control of our lives is often like trying to squeeze a wet bar of soap. We weren't created to direct God to our location; we were designed to serve God for His purposes. In fact, the more we force our own will, the more we push God away. If we truly believed that we are His creatures, we need not fear life. We would all sleep better if we felt safe in the arms of God. Like my college days experience, couples need to be available for His spirit to direct them. The conviction to become broken before God and trust him with your life and marriage is the obvious starting point for spiritual intimacy.

### *The Seed of Holiness*

This seed epitomizes the belief that the best thing you can do for your relationship is to demonstrate the highest standard of living yourself. Holiness can be defined as being morally blameless. God proclaims that He is holy and challenges his creatures to be holy. Moral integrity is contagious and influential in the lives of others. Relationships are built by joining two individuals; therefore each person's contributions directly impact the relationship. Imagine baking a cake with spoiled milk. You may have all the best ingredients to bake a sweet cake, yet spoiled milk would contaminate the whole process and change the outcome.

Likewise, a person's lifestyle will impact a marriage. I am frequently reminded of the "spoiling" addictions can cause in relationships. An alcoholic husband can destroy his marriage without his wife even knowing that he drinks. His lifestyle choice creates both subtle and overt rifts in the flow of marriage connection. The temptation to pursue happiness rather than holiness can cause a chain reaction. Couples centered on pleasure can be immobilized by their insatiable desires. On the other hand, pursuing a life authentically committed to holy living cultivates better connections and relational habits. If you desire an authentic soul connection with your spouse, then conduct yourself with honor and integrity. The relationship will be enriched by your actions and your partner will be encouraged by your efforts and goodness.

### *The Seed of Openness*

Openness is comfortably sharing stories, insights, and struggles with your partner. These moments open the door for God to speak to your relationship. Without sharing, we cheat God of opportunities to let His words penetrate individual agendas. Each partner may hear Him separately; yet, never give him a moment to speak to the relationship. In those very moments, you can allow God to direct you, love you, and heal you as a couple. So many couples can't enjoy this connection because they don't risk sharing. You may find yourself broken and living a holy life, yet never really bonding with your mate because you lack openness.

I'm often confronted with my own problems with openness. My personality mask makes me appear very open. The reality is more complex. Several years ago, a colleague helped me realize my shortsightedness about this. When I feel most open, he reminds me that I enjoy dancing in front of crowds, yet don't know how to dance alone. He confronts my sense of openness by asking me a series of questions like, "What are you not saying to your wife that she needs to hear?" That question seems harmless until you find a list forming in your head. I am open about my own shortcomings and faults, but rarely open up about negative feelings toward my wife. If I have any negative feelings about my wife, I keep them to myself. Eventually, negative emotion leads to negative behavior. If I am to remain open to God and my wife, I must remain open on all levels, even those that are difficult. It's like opening a window to catch a breeze, you may also get humidity, noise, and a few bugs.

Marriage openness requires full disclosure. God more readily uses people who are open to Him. Remember little David and his slingshot? Or Noah building the Ark? Despite enormous obstacles, Mary's openness to God and to her betrothed, Joseph, gave us our salvation. Being open to each other and God is the right action to take. Like the road less traveled, it is not always desired nor easy but very true.

"May all your expectations be frustrated. May all your plans be thwarted. May all of your desires be withered into nothingness. That you may experience the powerlessness and poverty of a child and sing and dance in the love of God the Father, the Son and the Spirit." —*Blessings given to Henri Nouwen by his spiritual mentor*

**The Us Marriage Challenge**

Understanding the three marital types, developing the five C skills, and making the three significant connections, provides you with proven steps toward a fulfilling marriage. The way you interact with your spouse determines the level of intimacy you will have. When you master key relationship skills, you can enjoy marital growth and avoid unwanted distractions. As you deepen the connection to your relationship (mind), sexual intimacy (body), and your spirit (soul), you will begin to experience the marriage you always wanted.

If the Us marriage is what you desire, here are some guidelines that will assist you on your journey.

- What's good for the relationship is always good for you. What's good for you is not always what's good for the relationship.
- Learn to enjoy love from the relationship, rather than struggling to get love from the relationship.
- Contribute daily deposits into the relationship from your mind, body, and soul.

These guidelines will only be as effective as you are able to understand and practice the contents of this book. Trying to build an Us marriage without practicing would be like trying to run a marathon without training. If you are not married and desire to be someday, begin to practice these guidelines as early as possible in any relationships you begin. If you are married, you are involved in the most amazing and potentially rewarding human experience on the planet.

The sustaining power behind a life long, increasingly intimate, Christ-centered marriage, comes from investing your love in the relationship rather than each other.

SOUL MATES
Chapter Summary
RED
I am trying to be as good as I can be.
YELLOW
I will help you be the best you can be.
GREEN
We surrender to the relationship, because we alone can't be good enough.

# Notes

*Chapter 1: Traffic Light Marriages*

Robert Sternberg, "The Triangular Theory of Love," *Psychology Review* (1986): 119–135.

Paul Pearsall, *The Ten Laws of Lasting Love* (New York: Avon, 1993).

Ibid.

John Eldredge, *Wild at Heart* (Nashville: Nelson, 2001).

Nathaniel Branden, *The Six Pillars of Self-Esteem* (New York: Bantam, 1994).

*Chapter 2: The Collage of Compatibility*

Les and Leslie Parrott, *Relationships* (Grand Rapids: Zondervan, 1998).

Gary Smalley and John Trent, *The Two Sides of Love* (Colorado Springs: Focus on the Family, 1990).

*Chapter 3: Courageous Conversation*

Kahlil Gibran, *The Prophet* (New York: Alfred A. Knopf, 1955).

John M. Gottman, Ph.D., and Nan Silver, *The Seven Principles of Making Marriage Work* (New York: Three Rivers Press, 1999).

Matthew McKay, Ph.D., Martha Davis, Ph.D., and Patrick Fanning, *Messages* (Oakland, CA: New Harbinger, 1995).

Daniel Goleman, *Emotional Intelligence* (New York: Bantam, 1995).

John M. Gottman and Nan Silver, *The Seven Principles of Making Marriage Work.* Lewis B. Smedes, *The Art of Forgiving* (New York: Ballantine, 1996).

Howard J. Markman, Scott M. Stanley, and Susan L. Blumberg, *Fighting for Your Marriage* (San Francisco: Jossey-Bass, 1994).

Gary Smalley, *Making Love Last Forever* (Dallas: Word, 1996).

*Chapter 4: The Cooperation Challenge*

Rudolf Dreikurs, *Fundamentals of Adlerian Psychology* (Chicago: Alfred Adler Institute, 1953).

Leo Buscaglia, *Loving Each Other* (New York: Ballantine, 1984).

Nathaniel Brandon, *The Six Pillars of Self-Esteem* (New York: Bantam, 1994).

John Gottman and Nan Silver, *The Seven Principals for Making Marriage Work.*

Judith S. Wallerstein and Sandra Blakeslee, *The Good Marriage: How and Why Love Lasts* (Boston: Houghton Mifflin, 1995).

*Chapter 5: Commitment Capabilities*

Kristen Davis and Mary Beth Franklin, "Simplify Your Life," *Kiplinger's Personal Finance* (August 2001): 64.

The Message Bible

Alfred Adler, *What Life Should Mean To You* (NY: Capricorn Books, 1958).

Scott M. Stanley, *The Heart of Commitment* (Nashville: Thomas Nelson, 1998).

Theodore Millon, *Toward a New Personology* (New York: John Wiley and Sons, 1990).

Michael Jordan, *I Can't Accept Not Trying* (San Francisco: Harper Collins, 1994).

*Chapter 6: Comfortably Close*

David Olsen, "National Survey of Marital Strengths," *Smart Marriage Conference: Denver Colorado* (Keynote paper presentation, 2000).

Larry Crabb, *Inside Out* (Colorado Springs: Navpress, 1988).

Susan Heitler, *The Power of Two* (Oakland, CA: New Harbinger, 1997).

*Chapter 7: Love R Us*

Rudolf Dreikers, *Fundamentals of Adlerian Psychology* .

Terry D. Hargrave, *The Essential Humility of Marriage* (Phoenix: Zeig, Tucker, & Theisen, 2000).

Ibid.

*Chapter 8: Sex from the Us Position*

Terry D. Hargrave, *The Essential Humility of Marriage* .

*Chapter 9: Soul Mates*

John Ortberg, *The Life You've Always Wanted* (Grand Rapids: Zondervan, 1997).

Dan B. Allender and Tremper Longman III, *Intimate Allies,* (Wheaton, IL: Tyndale House, 1995).

Larry Crabb, *The Safest Place on Earth* (Nashville: Word, 1999).

# About the Author

Doug McKinley is a Licensed Clinical Psychologist, Life Coach and a certifiably interesting husband. He is a core faculty member of the Institute for Life Coach Training. He owns a group therapy practice and coaching business in Naperville, Illinois. He is frequently invited to hold marriage seminars and conducts *Mad About Us* seminars nationally. He has eighteen years of therapy experience, five years of marriage and leadership coaching, and has served as marriage director in three different churches. Doug's greatest passion is developing people to enjoy more meaningful relationships, from the inside out. His speaking style invites participants to listen for application rather than evaluation. He enjoys an incredible nineteen year marriage with his wife Jana, and has two fabulous children, Seth age twelve, and Megan age ten.

CPSIA information can be obtained at www.ICGtesting.com
Printed in the USA
LVOW120218111211

258689LV00001B/28/A